THE OFFICIAL iTV
F1 GRAND PRIX
GUIDE 1999

THIS IS A CARLTON BOOK

CLD21301
This edition published in 1999 for
Colour Library Direct
Godalming Business Centre
Woolsack Way
Godalming
Surrey GU7 1XW

10 9 8 7 6 5 4 3 2 1

A CIP catalogue record for this book is available
from the British Library

ISBN 1 84100 065 5

Project Editor: Roland Hall
Project Art Direction: Trevor Newman
Production: Sarah Schuman
Picture Research: Justin Downing

Printed and bound in Great Britain

The publisher has taken reasonable steps to
check the accuracy of the facts contained
herein at the time of going to press but can
take no responsibility for any errors.

THE OFFICIAL itv
F1 GRAND PRIX
GUIDE 1999

Bruce Jones

Colour
Library
Direct

CONTENTS

FOREWORD

MURRAY WALKER

How time flies when you're enjoying yourself! 1999 is the half-way point of ITV's five-year agreement to transform Britain's Grand Prix television coverage, and it has done a grand job with which I am mighty proud to be associated. Years one and two were full of drama with the championships going down to the wire; first Jacques Villeneuve and Michael Schumacher, and then Mika Hakkinen and Schumacher again, fought for the Drivers' title. ITV brought new insight to their battles with more background stories, more interviews and much more on-air time, while Carlton's praiseworthy Grand Prix Guide completed the ITV package with its penetrating look at the whole Formula One scene.

Now here we are with the prospect of a third stunning year. After a wonderful season, McLaren is back on top with another Constructors' Championship and Mika Hakkinen a very well-deserved new Number One. It certainly couldn't have happened to a nicer bloke, but will he be able to make it two in a row in 1999? Not without a long, hard struggle, for not only will his talented team-mate David Coulthard be out to defeat him, but Michael Schumacher will be striving even harder for his third title. With a winter of development behind the Ferrari, which so nearly got the job done in 1998, I wouldn't like to bet on the outcome.

And that's not all, for there are intriguing changes to the mix. Double American Champ Car title-winner Alex Zanardi is returning to Formula One to team up with Michael Schumacher's brother, Ralf, at Williams; and Heinz-Harald Frentzen is switching to Jordan to partner Damon Hill, who won so dramatically in Belgium last year and who could do even better in 1999. Will Ferrari let the loyal Eddie Irvine win? Only if it doesn't affect Schumacher's chances! But it could happen. How will the new BAR team perform with Williams refugee Jacques Villeneuve at the wheel? Can Benetton regain its former glory? Will the outclassed Prost, Arrows, Stewart and Minardi teams be able to make a better showing, and how will the common use of Bridgestone tyres affect the competition? With four World Champions battling for supremacy, there are a lot of fascinating questions to be answered.

One thing is for sure. I'm going to love every second of it. With our enthusiastic help, I hope you do, too!

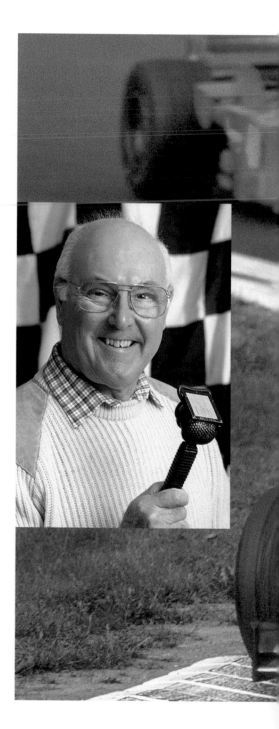

F1

ANALYSIS OF THE 1999 GRAND PRIX SEASON

McLAREN

BACK ON TOP

McLaren walked off with both the drivers' and manufacturers' titles last year, confirming that this famous team is back on top. And there's no reason to think that its drivers Mika Hakkinen and David Coulthard can't dominate again, but it should be closer still.

THE VIPs

Ron Dennis

Started as a mechanic with Cooper, but don't remind him of this. Rose to top with Rondel then Project Four Formula Two teams, then bought McLaren in early 1980. Took Formula One to new heights of professionalism, winning seven constructors' cups by 1991. Company also builds world-beating F I GTR sportscar.

Adrian Newey

Considered the top designer in Formula One, specialising in aerodynamics, Newey quit Williams at end of 1996 after a hugely successful spell was brought to an end by internal politics and joined McLaren. Started in Formula One with Fittipaldi then moved on to March, Force and Leyton House before joining Williams.

McLaren moved the goal posts in 1998 in such a major fashion that the other teams were left standing in the blocks as the McLaren men cruised to victory in the opening race at Melbourne by more than a lap. And the word "cruised" is used advisedly, as neither driver appeared to be pushing hard. Quite simply, the team had done its homework best over the winter, Adrian Newey had designed a car that made the most of the new grooved rubber and narrow-track regulations, and these two factors combined with Mercedes' strong engines and the talented driver line-up of Mika Hakkinen and David Coulthard was enough to produce the perfect result. Then, unlike in 1997, it proved not to be a false dawn and instead of following it up with a second win 12 races later as happened in 1997, the second 1998 win came at the second race. McLaren was back on top for the first time since 1991 and the rest had to pull out all the stops in a desperate attempt to catch up.

What became clear from that race in Australia was that there was precious little between the two drivers, with Coulthard honouring a pre-race agreement that whoever led into the first corner

WINNING TEAM: Ron Dennis greets his champion Hakkinen

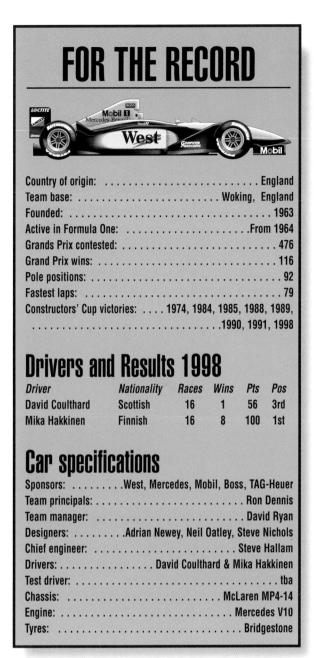

TALKING TACTICS: Ron Dennis and McLaren designer Adrian Newey consider the options and leave absolutely nothing to chance in their quest for glory

Schumacher back into the championship race.

However, while McLaren are seen as many things – not winning favour with their paranoid attitude to people looking into their garage shown by their security guards at every entrance – everyone in the team is a fighter. And this was shown with perfect clarity when Hakkinen produced his greatest drive to score his come-from-behind victory at the penultimate race, the Luxembourg Grand Prix at the Nurburgring.

Then came the World Championship shoot-out with Schumacher at Suzuka when Hakkinen kept his cool while Schumacher lost his. Needing only a second place to be sure of the title, Hakkinen won, while Schumacher started from the back and was then accounted for by a blowout. And this set the normally taciturn Finn singing in his cockpit with 19 laps still to run, his life's ambition having been achieved.

Same again please

Looking to the season ahead, Hakkinen is on board for a seventh campaign with McLaren, while Coulthard stays on for a fourth. And, in this pair, the team has two of the fastest drivers. In Mercedes, McLaren also has one of the strongest engines on offer. But the strongest card in the McLaren hand will again be ace designer Adrian Newey at the head of McLaren's renowned design team. Perhaps his impact won't be as great with his second McLaren, but this won't be due to a lack of input, merely that he doesn't have an all-new set of technical regulations around which to weave his magic.

There are many approaches to running a racing team, but no-one can be more involved than Ron Dennis, who appears to have a hand in everything. He frets, paces up and down, worries, holds out the arrow to indicate where the drivers should turn in to their pit stops and was always first to dive back from the pitwall if there was a problem during the race, such as when Coulthard's refuelling rig failed to work during the French Grand Prix. He lives and breathes the team. He is McLaren, soaring with the highs and plummeting with the lows. Yet this is what gives the team its 100 per cent approach. Mind you, as Ferrari's Ross Brawn showed when he guided Schumacher to victory at the Hungaroring last August with an inspired decision during the race to change his strategy from a two-stopper to a three-stopper, perhaps a rather more focused approach would make McLaren better still.

would have priority to win the race, later slowing to allow Hakkinen back in front after the Finn dropped out of the lead to make an erroneous pit stop. It seemed like a gallant gesture at the time, such was their dominance, but those extra four points for Hakkinen were to become considerably more important than they would have thought at the time.

Hakkinen asserted control in the second race, in Brazil, and thereafter moved into the dominant position in the team, although many felt that he was already seen as the team's number one due to his close personal relationship with team owner Ron Dennis. However, while there were days when Coulthard had the edge, Hakkinen was soon ahead on points and stayed there, with subsequent attention focused on him, particularly when the World Championship battle with Ferrari's Michael Schumacher heated up.

If the team's dominant one-two at Melbourne was a defining moment, so too were one-two at the Spanish Grand Prix, Hakkinen's runaway win at Monaco, and their back-to-back doubles in the Austrian and German Grands Prix. However, there were downsides, too, with a tactical blunder that let an inspired Schumacher win the Hungarian Grand Prix and considerably more mechanical failures than were suffered by Ferrari, with a double retirement at the Canadian Grand Prix opening the door to let

MIKA HAKKINEN

A CHAMPION AT LAST

Mika Hakkinen started last season having finally won a Grand Prix and ended it as World Champion for his beloved McLaren team. Now he's back for more, and his confidence will know no bounds.

NUMBER ONE: Mika Hakkinen worked well with team-mate David Coulthard in 1998. Will they work so well together when both are going for gold in 1999?

Anyone who saw the way in which the McLarens dominated the opening rounds of 1998 will have found it hard to comprehend that Hakkinen had to wait until the final race before landing the title ahead of Ferrari's Michael Schumacher. But that, for assorted reasons and no little bad luck on the Finn's side, is what happened.

At Suzuka he displayed his extraordinary cool to lead from start to finish, while Schumacher stalled and had to start from the back, perhaps proving that Mika was the tougher under pressure. It was a just result, as his talents had gone unrewarded for too long. Indeed, before Mika made his Formula One debut in 1991, he was acknowledged as being the best driver outside the big league, better even than Michael Schumacher. He was also better than any driver that his Formula Three team boss, Dick Bennetts, had seen since former charge Ayrton Senna.

Looking at last year's form, Mika was handed the first race in Australia by team-mate David Coulthard after coming in for a pit stop when he hadn't been asked to. He then dominated in Brazil and was second in Argentina, but ominously this was behind Schumacher. Then mechanical failure struck at Imola. But this was a minor blip as Mika stormed the next two races at Barcelona and Monaco. He retired again in Montreal, and with Schumacher winning, this was a double blow. That the Ferraris were first and second in France was another knock to Mika's confidence as he trailed them home in third. And losing at Silverstone, largely because the deployment of the safety car after torrential rain cost him a 40-second lead, was a real body blow.

But Mika bounced back with wins in Austria and Germany. Two mechanical failures and an accident gave him four points from the next three races, but Mika responded with his greatest race at the Nurburgring, where victory took him to that final round with a four-point advantage.

A Flying Finn

A multiple Finnish karting champion, Mika moved up to Formula Ford in 1987, doing even better than his fellow Finn, JJ Lehto, had done in 1986 by taking a clean sweep of the Finnish, Swedish and Nordic titles. He was then European Formula Opel Champion in 1988, and won the British Formula Three title in 1990 after a scrap with compatriot Mika Salo. Lotus signed him for 1991.

There have been setbacks since then, such as not getting to compete in 1993 until the final three Grands Prix after a gamble to join McLaren from Lotus went wrong; Senna had decided not to retire, and Mika became the third driver in a two-car team behind Senna and Indycar convert Michael Andretti. When Mika did step up, he shocked everyone by outqualifying Senna at Estoril. Yet, amazingly it took until the last race of 1997, at Jerez, before he scored his first Grand Prix win. However, no one who drove for McLaren in the mid-1990s stood a chance of winning. Consider, too, that Mika came close to death after suffering major head injuries by crashing in Australia in 1995.

DAVID COULTHARD

TIME TO CONSOLIDATE

David Coulthard was perfectly positioned to be champion in 1998, but the results went team-mate Mika Hakkinen's way and so did McLaren's support. However, he stands an excellent chance of succeeding this year.

blew. So it was a year of immense promise that turned into one of frustration.

A flying Scotsman

Having a father who raced karts meant that young David was racing by the time he was eight. And he hit the ground running when he moved to Formula Ford in 1989. In fact, he so impressed that McLaren and Autosport magazine launched a scholarship, with the prize of a run in a McLaren... David was second to Rubens Barrichello in the 1991 British Formula Three Championship, going on to win the prestigious Macau street race. Then the money ran out and, despite winning once in Formula 3000, all momentum looked lost as he accepted a test driver's role at Williams for 1994.

But Ayrton Senna's death propelled David into the big time, with his first win coming in the 1995 Portuguese Grand Prix, followed by victory in the 1997 Australian Grand Prix, which put McLaren back on the winning track.

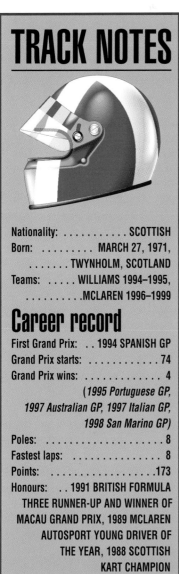

TRACK NOTES

Nationality: . . . . SCOTTISH
Born: . . . . MARCH 27, 1971,
. . . . TWYNHOLM, SCOTLAND
Teams: . . . . . WILLIAMS 1994–1995,
. . . . .MCLAREN 1996–1999

Career record

First Grand Prix: . . 1994 SPANISH GP
Grand Prix starts: 74
Grand Prix wins: 4
*(1995 Portuguese GP,
1997 Australian GP, 1997 Italian GP,
1998 San Marino GP)*
Poles: 8
Fastest laps: 8
Points: 173
Honours: . . 1991 BRITISH FORMULA
THREE RUNNER-UP AND WINNER OF
MACAU GRAND PRIX, 1989 MCLAREN
AUTOSPORT YOUNG DRIVER OF
THE YEAR, 1988 SCOTTISH
KART CHAMPION

David Coulthard is a cool operator. Few events proved this more clearly than last year's Australian Grand Prix, when he found himself leading after Hakkinen mistakenly pitted, yet honoured an agreement that whichever of them led into the first corner would win the race, letting Hakkinen by in the final laps. Cool and honourable, certainly, but it also gave Hakkinen the upper hand, and he never let go.

In truth, Hakkinen outperformed David more times than the other way around, but there often wasn't a lot in it. And while people say that Eddie Irvine was a dutiful number two to Michael Schumacher at Ferrari, David was even more dutiful at McLaren, as he at least had equal equipment. David is sure to be hoping that 1999 will be payback time with McLaren, and that he will be able to get his nose ahead and keep Hakkinen in his wake.

Second places in the first two Grands Prix last year should have been followed by victory at Buenos Aires. But he was tipped out of the lead by Schumacher and fell to sixth. He made amends by winning at Imola. Second behind Hakkinen in Barcelona should have been followed by second at Monaco, but his engine blew. Then the Canadian Grand Prix should have been his, but more mechanical failures saw him join Hakkinen in retirement. A jammed fuel rig ruined his French Grand Prix, and a spin into retirement at Silverstone left him with a red face. But his drive of the year came in Austria, when he was caught up in a first-lap incident and pitted for a new nose before tearing through the field to second. However, his most galling race must have been at Monza, where he was in control until his engine

READY FOR GLORY: David Coulthard played the number two role, but wants to be number one

FERRARI

A SERIOUS CHALLENGE

Ferrari was made to fight last year by McLaren's outstanding regeneration. And fight it did, Michael Schumacher taking the title race to the final round. This year Ferrari means to go one better and put itself back on top.

CALLING THE SHOTS: Ross Brawn controls Ferrari's winning tactics from the pitwall during the races

Ferrari has come within an ace of having one of its drivers crowned World Champion in both of the past two seasons, with Michael Schumacher losing out both at Jerez in 1997 and at Suzuka in 1998, first to Jacques Villeneuve and then to Mika Hakkinen. But expect the world's most famous team to come back all the stronger in the season ahead, with Ferrari president Luca di Montezemolo stating that Ferrari is "certain" to win the title in 1999.

After all, a team with a seemingly unlimited budget, fantastic engines and tip-top reliability simply has to win the World Championship. Especially if that team has Schumacher driving its lead car, producing the sort of performances that have marked him out as the driver to beat in the second half of the 1990s. Winning the World Championship is a matter of huge importance to Ferrari, though, as 20 years have passed since the marque last produced a World Champion, in Jody Scheckter in 1979, and 15 years since its cars have won the Constructors' Cup.

Di Montezemolo used to trot out the line that the year ahead would see the team aiming to win a handful of races in preparation for an all-out attack on the championship the following year. However, that changed last season, and Fiat supremo Gianni Agnelli deemed that if Ferrari failed to

win the World Championship with Schumacher, then the team would have failed the German.

Well, this they did, but their only failure can have been to have started with a car that wasn't as suited to the new narrow-track, grooved rubber rules as well as the rival McLarens. The team can't be faulted on its efforts to make up ground, with Rory Byrne's design team not seeing the light of day as it produced one aerodynamic tweak after another. Technical director Ross Brawn worked ceaselessly with tyre suppliers Goodyear to take the battle to McLaren and Bridgestone, while sporting director Jean Todt kept his hand on the tiller to keep everyone calm and focused in this once volatile Italian team. Indeed, its success was down to a South African, an Englishman and a Frenchman, plus its German and Northern Irish drivers...

So near, and yet...

The shock experienced by McLaren's rivals after they were all trounced at Melbourne made many consider giving up. But Ferrari was not among them, even though Schumacher had pulled off with engine failure when third, and team-mate Eddie Irvine could finish only a lapped fourth behind Heinz-Harald Frentzen's Williams. They were then thumped again at Interlagos, but this time the gap to Schumacher in third was less than a lap.

Goodyear introduced a wider front tyre for the Argentinian GP and this, combined with an aggressive drive from Schumacher, produced a victory. When Schumacher harried David Coulthard's McLaren for victory in the

FOR THE RECORD

Country of origin: .... Italy
Team base: .... Italy
Founded: 1939
Active in Formula One: .... From 1950
Grands Prix contested: 603
Grand Prix wins: 119
Pole positions: 124
Fastest laps: 133
Constructors' Cup victories: 1961, 1964, 1975, 1976,
.... 1977, 1979, 1982, 1983

Drivers and Results 1998

Driver	Nationality	Races	Wins	Pts	Pos
Eddie Irvine	Northern Irish	16	0	47	4th
Michael Schumacher	German	16	6	86	2nd

Car specifications

Sponsors: .... Marlboro, Shell, Pioneer, Asprey
Team principals: .... Jean Todt
Team manager: .... Ross Brawn
Designer: .... Rory Byrne
Chief engineer: .... Giorgio Ascanelli
Drivers: .... Michael Schumacher and Eddie Irvine
Test driver: .... tba
Chassis: .... Ferrari F300
Engine: .... Ferrari V10
Tyres: .... Bridgestone

San Marino GP, Ferrari seemed to be back in the hunt, especially as Irvine finished third. But any such thoughts were dispelled when McLaren's drivers dominated next time out, in Spain. Monaco was another rout, although Irvine salvaged third.

Then the circus went to Canada and a double McLaren failure opened the door for Schumacher, even though he had to make up for a stop-go penalty before taking the chequered flag. Two more wins followed at Magny-Cours and Silverstone to put Schumacher right up with Hakkinen. However, the second of these was extremely fortunate, as a procedural mistake by the officials allowed him to take a stop-go penalty in the pit lane after crossing the finish line.

When McLaren got its act together and rattled off one-two finishes in Austria and Germany, it seemed as though the battle was beyond Ferrari. But Brawn guided Schumacher to the win of the year at the Hungaroring, this a tactical tour de force. Ferrari will want to forget Schumacher slamming into Coulthard when lapping him in the Belgian GP, but it will always recall Schumacher leading Irvine home for a Monza one-two to draw level with Hakkinen. While that race was one Ferrari hadn't expected to win, it was confident that it could beat Hakkinen at the Nurburgring, but was shocked when Hakkinen came out ahead. And despite claiming pole at Suzuka, Schumacher made the one mistake of his season: he stalled and had to start from the back, ending all realistic hopes of usurping Hakkinen. Then, despite charging through to third, a blow-out ended it all.

Built around Schumacher

Schumacher's superior skills have turned Ferrari from a team that won once in a blue moon to one that has a chance at every circuit. He won six times last season and five times in 1997, two up on his 1996 haul and just two fewer than Villeneuve's title-clinching tally, but it has to be said that Ferrari didn't deserve this total, for it was occasionally Schumacher who won the race rather than Ferrari. After all, Irvine has only come close to winning once in his three years with the team, when he pushed Villeneuve to the finish in Argentina in 1997

PREPARED FOR ACTION: The Ferrari pit crew, one of the best in the business, steels itself for the crucial 10 second flurry of activity that is a pitstop

MICHAEL SCHUMACHER

A MAN FOR ALL SEASONS

Michael Schumacher may have been thwarted in his bid to win the 1998 world title for Ferrari. However, expect him to be back in the thick of things in 1999, out to prove that he is the world's greatest driver of all time.

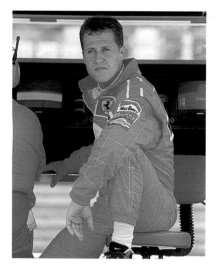

ALWAYS THINKING: Michael Schumacher doesn't miss a trick

Michael Schumacher failed to become a three-time World Champion last year. But his performance was perhaps greater than any he has produced before, even in his title-winning seasons of 1994 and 1995.

Last year was one in which Ferrari had to have a shot at the title – not just for their credibility, but also to hold on to Michael. And they didn't start in style, as their cars were left gasping by the pace of the McLarens. But wider Goodyear tyres made a difference in Argentina, and Michael did the rest.

He had no regular answer to the McLarens, though, and it wasn't until Canada that he won again after the McLarens had both retired. Wins in France and Britain followed, the latter being rather fortuitous as he served a stop-go penalty after crossing the finish line. Michael's victory in Hungary was a masterpiece, but throwing away victory by crashing into Coulthard at Spa was not. He benefited from a Hakkinen problem to win at Monza, but being outraced at the Nurburgring left him with a four-point deficit going to Suzuka. Pole position gave him hope, but stalling meant that he had to start from the back of the grid, and all hopes were blown – as was his tyre, after a charge up to third place.

Racing up the ladder

Michael was a karting ace who was guided into car racing by mentor Willi Weber. He tried Formula Three in 1989, winning the German title and the prestigious Macau street race in 1990 after a last-lap clash with Hakkinen. He was also a sportscar driver for Mercedes. Michael made his Formula One debut for Jordan in Belgium in 1991, then was traded by Benetton for its second driver, Roberto Moreno, and the points flowed.

Michael scored his first win in Belgium in 1992. Another win followed in 1993, but it all came right when he won eight times in 1994, despite being prevented from starting two races as a result of an unsuccessful appeal against exclusion from the British GP. It came to a head in Australia, when he clipped a wall and took both himself and Damon Hill out. In so doing, he claimed the title. His 1995 title was claimed in a more acceptable manner as he pursued Hill's superior Williams, and came out with nine wins to Hill's four. Racing for Ferrari in 1996, Michael won three times to be third overall. Five wins followed in 1997, but his title hopes were dashed when he crashed into Jacques Villeneuve in the final race at Jerez.

EDDIE IRVINE

SCHUEY'S LITTLE HELPER

Eddie Irvine would love to be a number one driver, but only with a top team. So, for now, he's happy to remain as number two to Michael Schumacher at Ferrari. But he must start winning races to preserve his reputation.

Eddie Irvine had his most successful Formula One season last year, finishing on the podium eight times as he raced to fourth place overall in the championship. But he never won a race, or even came close to doing so, while team-mate Michael Schumacher won on six occasions.

However, it would be harsh to judge Eddie as an under-achiever, as Ferrari is geared around the German, with Eddie very much a number two who takes whatever is left. Scan the results closely, though, and it's clear that there were days when Eddie matched Schumacher for pace. And if Schumacher is seen as the class of the field, then it means that Eddie is no slouch. In the races, though, the only area in which he outshone Schuey was at race starts.

Perhaps the only way to gauge Eddie's merits is for him to move to another team as its number one, which will also shake off the notion some people have that he's in racing only for the money.

Looking back at last year, Eddie had collected four third places and then a second at Magny-Cours by the midpoint – with his performance in the French Grand Prix the most useful, as he held the McLarens behind while Schumacher escaped to victory. He was second again in the Italian and Japanese Grands Prix, but was often on the podium as a result of McLaren failures. Indeed, he was criticized for letting Hakkinen through into second so easily in the Luxembourg Grand Prix.

In the beginning

Eddie won the 1987 British Formula Ford title and Festival. A frontrunner in Formula Three, he graduated to Formula 3000 in 1989. Driving for Eddie Jordan Racing in 1990, Eddie came third overall, ahead of Damon Hill and Heinz-Harald Frentzen. He raced in Formula 3000 in Japan for three years, ending up as runner-up in 1993. It was at the end of 1993 that he was given his Formula One break at Suzuka, racing for Jordan. Immediately he upset the order, when he shone in the race by finishing sixth and was later punched by Ayrton Senna, who thought Eddie had been blocking him.

Two subsequent years with Jordan saw him prove that he had the racing acumen to match his speed, and the way in which he got the better of team-mate Rubens Barrichello was one of the reasons why he was able to move to Ferrari in 1996. The first race at Melbourne was a false dawn as he finished third. He scored points in two of the next four Grands Prix, but then retired from the next nine races. Luckily, he was able to end 1996 on a more upbeat note, no doubt praying that 1997 would be more fruitful. Despite chasing Jacques Villeneuve to the line in Argentina and collecting four third places, it wasn't to be.

TRACK NOTES

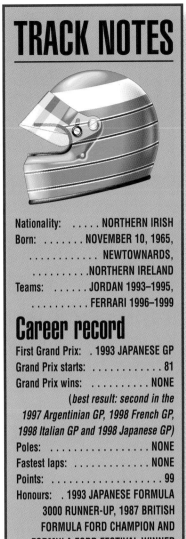

Nationality:	NORTHERN IRISH
Born:	NOVEMBER 10, 1965,
	NEWTOWNARDS,
	NORTHERN IRELAND
Teams:	JORDAN 1993–1995,
	FERRARI 1996–1999

Career record

First Grand Prix:	1993 JAPANESE GP
Grand Prix starts:	81
Grand Prix wins:	NONE

(best result: second in the 1997 Argentinian GP, 1998 French GP, 1998 Italian GP and 1998 Japanese GP)

Poles:	NONE
Fastest laps:	NONE
Points:	99
Honours:	1993 JAPANESE FORMULA 3000 RUNNER-UP, 1987 BRITISH FORMULA FORD CHAMPION AND FORMULA FORD FESTIVAL WINNER

WILLIAMS

SET FOR A THIN YEAR

THE VIPs

Frank Williams
Raced in Formula Three until he turned to team ownership in 1969, running a Formula One Brabham for Piers Courage. Struggled with lack of budget until landing Saudi backing in late 1970s, and has since won nine Constructors' Cups. Confined to a wheelchair since being crippled in road accident in 1986.

Patrick Head
The son of a gentleman racing driver, Patrick started as a designer at Lola in 1970 and progressed via various projects to become Frank Williams's partner in Williams Grand Prix Engineering in 1976, designing FW07 chassis with which Alan Jones won the 1980 world title. Now more involved with operations than design.

Reigning constructors' cup champions Williams fell from grace in 1998. And this season promises to be little better as the new recruits have an engine that is unlikely to let them trouble Ferrari and McLaren.

If continuity is one of the keys to success in Formula One, then Williams has a troubled season ahead, with two new drivers in Ralf Schumacher and Alessandro Zanardi. So, predicting its form is something of a lottery. However, one thing is for sure: team owners Frank Williams and Patrick Head will be expecting a far better season than they endured in 1998, when they slipped from first in the Constructors' Cup to third. A few points less, and they would have fallen to fifth.

Entering last year's World Championship as the champion team, and armed with World Champion Jacques Villeneuve and the driver who was classified second in 1997, Heinz-Harald Frentzen, one could only predict that Williams would be setting the pace again. Indeed, this English-to-the-core team had dominated Formula One in the 1990s, and there was no reason to think that its victorious momentum would be interrupted. After all, nothing breeds success like success.

However, last year we predicted that there were two reasons for thinking what some considered the unthinkable. Firstly, there was a new set of regulations, making the teams field narrower cars on grooved tyres, which caused completely new thinking in chassis design. And whenever the designers are set a new challenge like this, it upsets the applecart, as one designer produces a tweak that sets his cars apart. Invariably that designer is from one of the top teams, maintaining that status quo with the other teams taking a while to catch up. However, on 1997's form, Williams no longer had the best design team, as design leader Adrian Newey had

GIVING HIS ALL: World Champion Jacques Villeneuve could do nothing to protest his title and has left the team

gone to McLaren. Indeed, although Newey was responsible for the design of the 1997 Williams FW19, he didn't stay and help develop it, and the way in which the other teams caught up was proof that a designer should also be responsible for a car's ongoing development.

The second concern was that Williams took its eye off the ball in 1997, concentrating more than their drivers would have liked on getting a car developed for last year's incoming regulations rather than focusing on keeping the FW19 ahead of the field. And, as history now relates, this work did not reap dividends.

Long faces

Indeed, in 1998, there were no Williams victories and Villeneuve and Frentzen shared three podium visits between them, the Canadian finishing third twice and Frentzen third once. When you consider that third place for a Williams driver was considered something of a failure in 1997 – yet 12 months later it was thought of as a success – it wasn't surprising that the Williams garage was home to some of the longest faces in the pit lane.

Amazingly, one of the few who kept cheery was none other than Villeneuve, and he didn't find his entertainment just by changing his hair

POWER TALKS: Team supremos Patrick Head and Frank Williams confer on how to make their cars go faster. They did a great deal of talking in 1998

colour from race to race. No, he showed yet again that he simply loved driving racing cars, and he never gave less than his best in a car that often looked more than a handful. Time and again he proved that he is a real racer, leaving his team-mate in his wake once the races got underway.

And what made his press-on approach all the more commendable was that he knew for most of the season that he was heading off for pastures new in 1999, when he would join up with his mentor Craig Pollock at the new BAR team and be joined by his long-time race engineer Jock Clear.

Frentzen often cut something of a forlorn figure, although his relationship with the team was clearly better than it had been in 1997. However, he still failed to come up to scratch, enduring a fruitless middle third to his season. It's now up to Jordan to see if they can coax him into making the most of his undoubted speed.

New blood

So, what will the new boys bring to the team? Schumacher will bring the experience gained in two seasons at Jordan, in which he has displayed great speed but not a little indiscipline. And while Williams has employed him for the former attribute, it certainly won't accept displays of the latter.

Zanardi, on the other hand, has spent three years away from Formula One after a troubled time predominantly with Lotus. That he is returning to Formula One with two Indycar titles to his name shows how extraordinarily fruitful his time has been on the North American scene. And it was during this time that he established a firm reputation for being a fierce competitor who takes no prisoners. Add this fighter's edge to his renowned technical abilities, and this is precisely what the Williams management is after as the team endures an interim season with its Supertec customer Renault engines before the arrival of its BMW engines for the 2000 season.

With several of the team's lower management strata leaving for pastures new over the winter, Patrick Head will have to work hard to pull the new strands together, while hoping that his design team headed by Gavin Fisher and Geoff Willis can come up with a fantastic chassis, as, come what may, the Mecachrome engine is expected to give away vital horsepower to the Mercedes, Ferrari and Mugen Honda engines used by some of their rivals.

FOR THE RECORD

Country of origin:	England
Team base:	Grove, England
Founded:	1968
Active in Formula One:	From 1973
Grands Prix contested:	395
Grand Prix wins:	103
Pole positions:	108
Fastest laps:	110
Constructors' Cup victories:	1980, 1981, 1986, 1987, 1992, 1993, 1994, 1996, 1997

Drivers and Results 1998

Driver	Nationality	Races	Wins	Pts	Pos
Heinz-Harald Frentzen	German	16	0	17	7th
Jacques Villeneuve	Canadian	16	0	21	5th

Car specifications

Sponsors:	Winfield, Castrol
Team principals:	Frank Williams
Technical director:	Patrick Head
Team manager:	Dickie Stanford
Chief engineer:	James Robinson
Drivers:	Alessandro Zanardi and Ralf Schumacher
Test driver:	tba
Chassis:	Williams FW21
Engine:	Supertec V10
Tyres:	Bridgestone

ALESSANDRO ZANARDI

READY FOR A SECOND TRY

Alessandro Zanardi tried Formula One and came away with nothing. Then he rebuilt his career in the USA, winning two Indycar titles. And now he's back looking to win with Williams.

THE SECOND COMING: Alessandro Zanardi aims to win on his return

'Alex' Zanardi is a driver who looked set never to be accorded the accolades his skills merited. You have only to look at the way in which Formula One treated him, and at his subsequent slip down to GT racing, to understand how wrong a driver's career can go. Luckily for him, he signed up with Chip Ganassi's Indycar team for 1996 and hasn't looked back since – to such an extent that he is back for his second crack at Formula One not only a far richer man, but also one who is able to walk into the lead drive of one of the teams that wouldn't so much as look at him when he sank from Formula One with Lotus at the end of 1994.

Alex was one of a host of Italians who shone in European kart racing circles and then progressed directly to Formula Three. Unlike many who make such a move, Alex was immediately quick in 1988, even trying his hand at Formula 3000 a year later. Back in Italian Formula Three in 1990, he ended up second overall, just as he did when Christian Fittipaldi outscored him to win the 1991 Formula 3000 crown. Formula One followed before that year was out, filling the seat Michael Schumacher had vacated at Jordan. Failure to land a ride in 1992 saw Alex contest only three Grands Prix, standing in at Minardi for the injured Fittipaldi.

A full-time ride was his for 1993 when he joined Lotus, scoring a point in his second race. But the team was on the slide, and his year was curtailed by a massive accident at Eau Rouge during practice for the Belgian GP. Back for more in 1994, matters became worse still, as a lack of finance finished the team off.

Re-born in the USA

After a brief spell with Lotus in GT racing, Alex signed to race in Indycars. And here he found his *métier*, winning four times to be third overall behind his Ganassi team-mate Jimmy Vasser and Michael Andretti in his rookie season. Five wins gave him the title in 1997 with a race still to run, and then he made it back-to-back titles in 1998 when six wins saw him crowned with four races still to run, by which time his ink was dry on his ticket back to Formula One: a Williams contract.

Acknowledged as a combative racer, having ruffled a few feathers in the less competitive Indycar arena, Alex is also one of the best test and development drivers. So he sounds precisely the sort of driver that Williams needs to lift its form in 1999.

TRACK NOTES

Nationality:	ITALIAN
Born:	OCTOBER 23, 1966
	BOLOGNA, ITALY
Teams:	JORDAN 1991,
	MINARDI 1992,
	LOTUS 1993–1994,
	WILLIAMS 1999

Career record

First Grand Prix:	1991 SPANISH GP
Grand Prix starts:	25
Grand Prix wins:	NONE
(best result: sixth, 1993 Brazilian GP)	
Poles:	NONE
Fastest laps:	NONE
Points:	1
Honours:	1998 INDYCAR CHAMPION,
	1997 INDYCAR CHAMPION,
	1996 INDYCAR ROOKIE OF THE YEAR,
	1991 FORMULA 3000 RUNNER-UP,
	1990 ITALIAN FORMULA 3 RUNNER-UP

RALF SCHUMACHER

READY TO BLOOM

Ralf Schumacher came of age as a driver in 1998 when he stopped crashing and used his natural speed to good effect for Jordan. But he wants more and for 1999 has moved to Williams, which may make or break him.

MEETING THE FANS: Ralf signs valued autographs at Silverstone

TRACK NOTES

Nationality: . . . . GERMAN
Born: . . . . JUNE 30, 1975,
 . . . . KERPEN, GERMANY
Teams: . . . . . . JORDAN 1997–1998,
 . . . . WILLIAMS 1999

Career record
First Grand Prix: 1997 AUSTRALIAN GP
Grand Prix starts: 33
Grand Prix wins: . . . . .NONE
(best result: second, 1998 Belgian GP)
Poles: . . . . NONE
Fastest laps: . . . . NONE
Points: 27
Honours: . . . 1996 FORMULA NIPPON
CHAMPION,
1995 GERMAN FORMULA THREE
RUNNER-UP, AND WON
1995 MACAU FORMULA THREE
GRAND PRIX

After a childhood spent racing on his father's karting circuit, Ralf Schumacher went directly to Formula Three in 1994, driving for the team owned by Willi Weber, Michael's mentor and manager. He scored his first win at the end of the season to end up third overall behind Jorg Muller and Alexander Wurz. Ralf had a straight fight with Norberto Fontana in 1995, with the Argentinian taking the honours. They met again in Formula Nippon (Japan's version of Formula 3000) in 1996, and Ralf was able to land the title at the final round, even though he crashed and had to wait until his team-mate Naoki Hattori also crashed and handed the title back to him. However, by then Ralf already had a Formula One contract in his pocket, from Jordan.

When Ralf arrived in Formula One in 1997, few outside the sport knew where he had come from. All they knew was that he was Michael's younger brother, and therefore that must be the only reason Jordan had signed him: the publicity

value. But Eddie also has an eye for talent, and he was feeling pleased with himself at the first race when Ralf was fifth fastest on the first day of practice. But he qualified 12th and was out after a lap. Two races later, in Argentina, he knocked team-mate Giancarlo Fisichella off, but atoned for this error by finishing third. Although Ralf scored points on five more occasions, he never finished so well again and was outraced and outpsyched by Fisichella. He also crashed too often, such as when he clashed with his brother at the first corner of the Luxembourg Grand Prix, all but sinking Michael's title hopes.

With Damon Hill as his team-mate in 1998, Ralf changed his approach, cleaning up his act after some wild moments in the early races. He also learned not to waste strong qualifying

performances with bad starts, and this came just as the team was pulling itself out of the mire. Indeed, not only did Ralf collect Jordan's first points at Silverstone, but he did so from the back row, making light of treacherous conditions. Then the points started to flow, although his display of petulance after being asked to stay behind Damon Hill in the closing laps of the Belgian GP, when the team didn't want to risk its first victory with internecine fighting, was telling. The fact that he was suing Jordan to release him from his contract probably didn't help...

Racing alongside Alex Zanardi at Williams will make Ralf or break him, as it's likely that team head Patrick Head will take to Alex ahead of Ralf. So Ralf will have to apply himself and, if this works, he could cause a major surprise.

JORDAN

ONE WIN ISN'T ENOUGH

Jordan broke into the big time last year with its first win. This year it plans to consolidate its position as one of the top teams, with two race winners filling its driver line-up.

It was a cruel twist of fate that when Jordan finally made its Formula One breakthrough by winning last year's Belgian Grand Prix, few people noticed, as the event had been dominated by the massive first-lap accident and then Michael Schumacher's clash with David Coulthard. More than that, Damon Hill was followed across the finish line by team-mate Ralf Schumacher, so not only was it the team's first victory but a one-two.

Yet, almost immediately, team owner Eddie Jordan wanted more. Yes, his team had joined the ranks of winners – as the 25th team to do so – but he felt disappointed that he hadn't felt more elated, and realized that overhauling both Williams and Benetton to be third in the Constructors' Cup would give more satisfaction. At the same meeting it became clear that Schumacher would be leaving the team after some legal wrangling. Jordan wasn't happy, yet, by the

following race at Monza, it was announced that team leader Hill was going to be joined for 1999 by Heinz-Harald Frentzen – meaning that Jordan would have two Grand Prix winners on its books. No longer would the team be seen as a kindergarten for drivers to attend while learning their trade before moving on to more established teams.

This also marked another stage in Jordan's development, as it meant that he could shake off the image of running a driver for his budget rather than his skills, a charge that Michael Schumacher levelled at his one-time boss when Ralf was struggling to leave the team.

So, this year must see everything come together. Look at the package and it's good, with a pair of quality drivers thanks to the backing of Benson & Hedges, Mugen Honda engines (which came on in leaps and bounds last season) and what should be an excellent chassis from Mike Gascoyne – the new man in the designer's hot seat since the departure of founding team member Gary Anderson.

MORE CHAMPAGNE PLEASE: Eddie Jordan luxuriates in the bubbly as supplied by Belgian GP winner Damon Hill

FOR THE RECORD

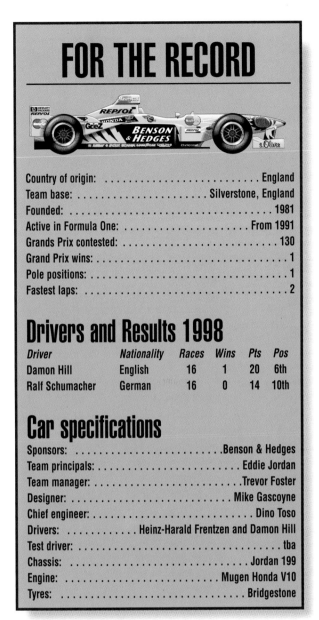

Country of origin:	England
Team base:	Silverstone, England
Founded:	1981
Active in Formula One:	From 1991
Grands Prix contested:	130
Grand Prix wins:	1
Pole positions:	1
Fastest laps:	2

Drivers and Results 1998

Driver	Nationality	Races	Wins	Pts	Pos
Damon Hill	English	16	1	20	6th
Ralf Schumacher	German	16	0	14	10th

Car specifications

Sponsors:	Benson & Hedges
Team principals:	Eddie Jordan
Team manager:	Trevor Foster
Designer:	Mike Gascoyne
Chief engineer:	Dino Toso
Drivers:	Heinz-Harald Frentzen and Damon Hill
Test driver:	tba
Chassis:	Jordan 199
Engine:	Mugen Honda V10
Tyres:	Bridgestone

PULLING POWER: Team sponsor Benson & Hedges furnished Jordan with glamour galore in 1998

A mixed history

When Jordan Grand Prix hit Formula One in 1991, it was a welcome addition and immediately looked a team that would last the pace, unlike so many that appeared in the late 1980s. Amazingly, before the year was out, Andrea de Cesaris had come close to giving the team its maiden victory when he was chasing Ayrton Senna's McLaren for the lead in the Belgian Grand Prix, until his engine blew with three laps to go. That race was also notable for a one-off drive by Michael Schumacher – his Formula One debut as a replacement for the recently jailed Bertrand Gachot – before Benetton secured him for the following race.

Fifth overall was an excellent first attempt, and earned Jordan a works engine deal for 1992. Sadly this was with Yamaha, and drivers Stefano Modena and Mauricio Gugelmin scored just one point. Paying for Hart engines in 1993 worked better and Rubens Barrichello starred at the third race, the European Grand Prix at Donington Park when he ran second behind Senna before retiring with fuel feed problems with six laps to go. The team's only points came when he and Eddie Irvine were fifth and sixth respectively in the penultimate race.

The 1994 season was far better and Jordan ranked fifth overall, Barrichello being third once and fourth five times. The following season produced a fantastic day for Jordan in Canada when Barrichello and Irvine

were second and third behind Alesi, who had raced for the team in Formula 3000. Sixth overall that year, they went one better in 1996, although neither Barrichello nor Martin Brundle made it on to the podium.

Ralf Schumacher shocked on his arrival in 1997, especially when he finished third in only his third Grand Prix and people started to realize he was more than just the brother of Michael Schumacher. However, the fact that he shunted team-mate Giancarlo Fisichella out of that race didn't impress. But the drivers settled down, and Fisichella finished fourth at Imola, sixth at Monaco and third at Montreal. Schumacher followed this with four races in the points. In Germany, Fisichella chased Gerhard Berger and briefly took the lead before suffering a puncture. Still, second at Spa brought the smile back, although this was wiped away when the pair clashed at the first corner at the Nurburgring.

The golden year

It all came right last year. But this breakthrough looked most unlikely in the first half of the season. And nowhere were the cars further from the pace than at Monaco, where whey lined up on the eighth row. Then a combination of Anderson producing a long-wheelbase chassis and Mugen Honda finding more horsepower helped Jordan turn the corner, with Ralf rushing from the back of the field in the wet to finish sixth at Silverstone.

Fifth next time out at the A1-Ring showed that this was no fluke. Then he chased the McLarens in third at Hockenheim, but was on a two-stop strategy and fell to sixth as Hill claimed fourth place. Hill was fourth again at the Hungaroring, and then came their day of days at Spa-Francorchamps. Both were in the points at Monza, with Ralf third to move right on to the tails of Williams and Benetton in their battle to end the year third overall. And Hill helped them displace Benetton from fourth position by finishing fourth at Suzuka.

DAMON HILL

BACK TO THE WINNER'S CIRCLE

A winner again in 1998, and this time not with Williams, Britain's 1996 World Champion Damon Hill will want to make winning a regular event in his second year with Jordan.

Damon Hill, they said, only won Grands Prix because he was a Williams driver. Well, he certainly put that myth to rest by giving Jordan its first win at Spa in 1998. Now he must win again to show that this was no fluke.

By winning the Drivers' World Championship in 1996, Damon Hill came out of the shadow of his double-World Champion father, the late Graham Hill. He fought charges of nepotism right from his first Formula Ford race in 1984, when he spun at almost every corner under the intense spotlight of the media. But Damon re-emerged in 1985 to become a front-runner. Three years of Formula Three competition produced four wins and a second place in the 1988 Formula Three Macau Grand Prix. Damon struggled to land a Formula 3000 drive, although he shone enough to become Williams's test driver. He made his Formula One debut for Brabham in 1992, then spent four years at Williams in a spell that produced his world title and 21 wins.

A step backwards

Yet, by the time he was World Champion he had been fired, and now his career is seen as a case of "life after Williams". Indeed, in 1997 he had a torrid time, as he was faced with the reality of driving for a lesser team – such had been the manner of his departure that he had little choice of drive, and thus ended up at Arrows. True, Tom Walkinshaw was the new man in command and the new Bridgestone tyres promised much, but little else did. When Damon scraped on to the grid for the opening race and broke down on the parade lap, there was genuine sympathy for his plight. Fortunately, things got better and he finally scored a point at Silverstone, then came within an ace of winning in Hungary. Against all form, he caught and passed Michael Schumacher's Ferrari, then shot away ahead of the German. But with three laps to go, his gearbox started to pack up and he was passed on the last lap by Jacques Villeneuve. In subsequent races, he returned to middle-order positions.

At the start of 1998, though, everything seemed to go wrong, with the Jordans struggling to keep clear of the backmarkers rather than challenging the front-runners. And nowhere was this more true than at Monaco, where he and Ralf Schumacher qualified on the eighth row of the grid. But huge strides were made, especially by engine supplier Mugen Honda, with the result that they scored their first points at the British Grand Prix and then pulled off a one-two in Belgium. Damon proved he was back, and that, despite approaching 40 years of age, he's far from finished – in spite of what some are saying, it's certainly not a case of 'cruise-to-collect'. In 1999, he plans to build on the progress Jordan made last year, and turn them into regular winners.

PROVEN WINNER: Damon Hill knows how to uncork Champagne

TRACK NOTES

Nationality: . . . . ENGLISH
Born: . . . . . . .SEPTEMBER 17, 1960,
. . . . HAMPSTEAD, LONDON
Teams: . . BRABHAM 1992, WILLIAMS
. . . . . 1993–1996, ARROWS 1997,
. . . . JORDAN 1998–1999

Career record

First Grand Prix: . . 1992 BRITISH GP
Grand Prix starts: 100
Grand Prix wins: 22
(*1993 Hungarian GP,
1993 Belgian GP, 1993 Italian GP;
1994 Spanish GP, 1994 British GP,
1994 Belgian GP, 1994 Italian GP,
1994 Portuguese GP, 1994 Japanese
GP; 1995 Argentinian GP, 1995 San
Marino GP, 1995 Hungarian GP, 1995
Australian GP; 1996 Australian GP,
1996 Brazilian GP, 1996 Argentinian
GP, 1996 San Marino GP, 1996
Canadian GP, 1996 French GP, 1996
German GP, 1996 Japanese GP, 1998
Belgian GP*)
Poles: 20
Fastest laps: 19
Points: 353
Honours: . . WORLD CHAMPION 1996

HEINZ-HARALD FRENTZEN

A NEW ENVIRONMENT

Heinz-Harald Frentzen's Williams dream never worked and is now over. But life in the friendlier atmopshere at Jordan could yet see this affable German unlock his undoubted natural speed and start winning races again.

TRACK NOTES

Nationality:	GERMAN
Born:	MAY 18, 1967,
	MONCHENGLADBACH, GERMANY
Teams:	SAUBER 1994–1996,
	WILLIAMS 1997–98,
	JORDAN 1999

Career record

First Grand Prix:	1994 BRAZILIAN GP
Grand Prix starts:	81
Grand Prix wins:	1
	(1997 San Marino GP)
Poles:	1
Fastest laps:	6
Points:	89
Honours:	1997 FORMULA ONE RUNNER-UP, 1989 GERMAN FORMULA THREE RUNNER-UP, 1988 GERMAN FORMULA OPEL CHAMPION, 1984 GERMAN JUNIOR KARTING CHAMPION

The irony won't have escaped some fans, but Heinz-Harald's team-mate at Jordan this year will be Damon Hill, the driver he replaced at Williams in 1997. Fortunately, there is no animosity between them, and it's up to Damon to prove that he can blow Heinz-Harald away in equal equipment, and up to Heinz-Harald not to let that happen.

Heinz-Harald won the 1988 German Formula Opel series. Second in the German Formula Three series in 1989, he joined Mercedes's sports-car squad, but quit to concentrate on Formula 3000. Success didn't come and after two years he went to Japan, where he won occasionally before being summoned to Formula One in 1994 by Sauber, for whom he peaked with third place at Monza in 1995.

Trouble within

Soon after his dream move to Williams in 1997, Heinz-Harald was aware that he wasn't popular with the management. Luckily, he won at Imola fourth time out, but this was his only victory, while team-mate Jacques Villeneuve gained six. The chief reason for Williams picking him over Hill for the 1997 season was that they felt he possessed more natural speed. However, this logic had been questioned during the second half of his final year with Sauber, when he was outpaced by Johnny Herbert in the team's second car. It was thought to be an attitude problem, and he was expected to be motivated at Williams. So, how can you explain his 1.75 second qualifying deficit to Villeneuve for the opening race?

To Heinz-Harald's credit, he wasn't swayed

SET TO SHINE: Heinz-Harald Frentzen is hoping to emerge from the shadows with Jordan

by criticism. All too often he would be involved in incidents, yet he insisted on being allowed to follow his own set-up thoughts and started to make progress. Victory in Hungary should have been his, but a mechanical problem intervened. He would have been in with a shout at the Luxembourg GP, too, but a coming-together with eventual winner Villeneuve at the first corner knocked off his ignition, and he fell to 13th place. At least a second place in Japan raised his profile, and five consecutive podium finishes helped Williams gain the constructors' title it so cherishes.

Last season saw an improvement in his relationship with the team, but still the results didn't come, with third place in the Australian GP his best showing. But it must be pointed out that the car wasn't up to Williams' usual standard. Whatever the case, he knew he wouldn't be required for 1999 and so started looking elsewhere, even considering a move to Indycars. However, at the Italian GP he pulled off a surprise by announcing that he would be joining Jordan.

BENETTON

A YEAR OF RECKONING

Last year was a disappointment for Benetton, but it was a year of transition, with the arrival of two new drivers and a new boss. Expect progress to be made in 1999, although the engine remains a weak link.

THE OUTGOING BOSS: David Richards was expected to lead the team forward but quit in 1998

Benetton boss David Richards said before last season was out that he thought that the team may have to wait four years before becoming competitive again. Now this won't have been music to the ears of drivers Giancarlo Fisichella and Alexander Wurz, but they know that however good the chassis may be, it won't go well until it has a strong works engine, and this is not due to happen until 2001. Even then, said Richards, it could take a further two seasons to start winning, as McLaren did once it had harnessed Mercedes power. However, there's a strong possibility that Benetton may get works Ford engines in 2000.

Whether Fisichella and Wurz are prepared to stay around that long remains to be seen, but their views may be coloured by the sudden departure of Richards in the middle of last October when he tendered his resignation, citing disappointment that the Benetton family was not keen to approve his three-year plans. In his place, 29-year-old Rocco Benetton will run the show, armed with the experience of working with the team for more than a year.

Seen as the underperformers of 1997, when they fielded the ultra-experienced pairing of Jean Alesi and Gerhard Berger, Benetton still finished third in the Constructors' Championship, thanks to the Frenchman's consistency and the Austrian's surprise victory in the German Grand Prix. However, last year saw them fall to fifth overall at the final round, with no wins to their credit as the drivers had to satisfy themselves with picking up the scraps from the big table occupied by McLaren and Ferrari.

A testament to youth

Losing works engines with the withdrawal of Renault at the end of 1997, and thus having to pay for the Renault-derived Mecachrome engines, precluded signing any of the established names. But, with Richards at the helm, pursuing a youth policy was always the likely way anyhow.

Fisichella arrived with a glowing reputation after a season that saw him win the battle of the rookies at Jordan, establishing himself ahead of Ralf Schumacher. Despite wanting to stay for 1998, a court ruled that the Italian must honour a contract with Benetton. And, to his credit, he got stuck in – no doubt relieved in the first half of the year when he collected points as the Jordans struggled. And nowhere was his fortune more clear than at Monaco, when he qualified third with the Jordans fifteenth and sixteenth, and then finished the race in second place. He was second again next time out in the Canadian Grand Prix, but thereafter the team's form dipped, even though he grabbed pole position for the Austrian Grand Prix as the wet track dried by the second, and he was the last driver to take the chequered flag in qualifying.

Wurz arrived with just three Grands Prix under his belt as a stand-in for Berger in the middle of 1997. The impact this young Austrian made was huge, as he outqualified Alesi at his second attempt (in France) and ran ahead of him for much of the race. He then shadowed

FOR THE RECORD

Country of origin:	England
Team base:	Enstone, England
Founded:	1986
Active in Formula One:	From 1986
Grands Prix contested:	267
Grand Prix wins:	27
Pole positions:	16
Fastest laps:	35
Constructors' Cup victories:	1995

Drivers and Results 1998

Driver	Nationality	Races	Wins	Pts	Pos
Giancarlo Fisichella	Italian	16	0	16	9th
Alexander Wurz	Austrian	16	0	17	7th=

Car specifications

Sponsors:	Benetton Sportsystem
Team principals:	Rocco Benetton
Team manager:	Joan Villadelprat
Designer:	Nick Wirth
Chief engineer:	Pat Symonds
Drivers:	Giancarlo Fisichella and Alexander Wurz
Test driver:	tba
Chassis:	Benetton B199
Engine:	Playlife V10
Tyres:	Bridgestone

Alesi throughout the British Grand Prix and finished third. Fortunately, he also did a huge amount of testing for the team, particularly concentrating on the new grooved tyres.

So he hit the ground running, finishing fourth in the second and third races in Brazil and Argentina. He collected a further fourth place in the Spanish Grand Prix. But he made his greatest impression when he was passed by Michael Schumacher at the Loews hairpin in the Monaco Grand Prix and promptly passed him back, showing that he's scared of no one. Mind you, next time out in Canada, Alesi had good reason to be scared of him as Alexander got involved in a first-corner squeeze and flew over the top of Alesi's Sauber before rolling through the gravel bed. Then, cool as you like, he jumped into the team's spare car for the restart. So both drivers had useful seasons, but will only progress if the team can give them the right equipment.

All about tyres

It wasn't just on the driving front that there had been changes, though, with a huge shake-up of the technical department after Michael Schumacher's departure for Ferrari in 1996. He was followed to the Italian team by designer Rory Byrne and master tactician Ross Brawn. This left Nick Wirth struggling in 1997 as he tried to discover why the car wouldn't get heat into its tyres. Then last year he had to pursue the route that most teams took in a bid to get their cars to work better on the grooved tyres, namely to lengthen the wheelbase mid-season.

However, the team's hopes of progress were stymied when tyre supplier Bridgestone concentrated on producing the tyre that suited McLaren best as they pitched for the title. This meant, for example, at Monza that while Benetton wanted the wider Bridgestone front tyres, only the narrower ones were brought, because this was what McLaren wanted. Benetton always put on a brave face, but it was a great frustration as they sought to develop the car. It was even more of a frustration when Goodyear appeared to move ahead in the tyre war in the second half of the season, helping not only Ferrari, but also Williams and Jordan, the two teams with whom Benetton was fighting for third place in the Constructors' Cup.

GIANCARLO FISICHELLA

A PRINCE IN WAITING

Ever since he started racing, it has been clear that Giancarlo Fisichella would become a major star. However, he is growing impatient for that breakthrough first Grand Prix win as he starts his second season with Benetton.

Giancarlo Fisichella was a karting legend in Italy. A year in Formula Alfa Boxer in 1991 led to three seasons in Italian Formula Three. Runner-up in the second year, he won the title in 1994, also winning at Monaco. But he didn't have the money for Formula 3000. Fortunately, Alfa Romeo beat Mercedes to sign him for the International Touring Car Championship, and Giancarlo spent two years in this multi-million pound high-tech arena. He was second in only his second race, while his results in 1996 were better still. But he was more interested in single-seaters and was Minardi's test driver in 1995, making his Formula One debut in 1996, contesting eight races and peaking with an eighth place in Canada before being replaced by 'rentadriver' Giovanni Lavaggi.

Eddie Jordan has an eye for rising talent, and when he fielded two young guns in 1997, he came up trumps with one of them: Giancarlo. Ironically, it was to Giancarlo that he bade farewell at the season's end, having lost a court case to try to prevent him from transferring to Benetton. Giancarlo didn't want to go, but he was duty bound by a management contract.

However, the impression he made at Jordan was huge. Slightly outpaced by team-mate Ralf Schumacher in the first race, he was ahead of him by the Argentinian Grand Prix and heading for a place on the podium, until he was knocked off by Ralf... But thereafter he was top dog, scoring points more often than not, while Ralf brought his car home on the back of the rescue truck.

Third place in the Canadian GP was overshadowed by leading half of the German GP, before ceding to Gerhard Berger and then having a punctured tyre flail against an oil line to put him out. So his best result was second place at Belgium, and Giancarlo had done enough to convince Italian racing fans that they finally had a star of their own again.

AN ITALIAN HERO: Giancarlo Fisichella carries the hopes of Italian fans on his shoulders

Life at Benetton promised so much in 1998, especially with the calm influence of David Richards at the helm, but as the year progressed it became clear that all Bridgestone's efforts were behind producing the right tyres for McLaren, and these tended not to be the ones that were best for Benetton. But still Giancarlo raced to second place in two successive races – at Monaco, and then in Montreal. He even made the most of a wet but drying track to grab pole for the Austrian GP, but the tail end of the season was a let-down. Provided Benetton can get its act together for the season ahead, however, you can be sure that Giancarlo will deliver.

ALEXANDER WURZ

THE NEXT GENERATION

Alexander Wurz is one of those people who does everything well and, as soon as Benetton provides him with a competitive package, he will deliver. It's just a question of when, not if.

Formula One was set to be overrun with jockey-sized drivers when Gerhard Berger retired, but along came Alexander Wurz, who not only was of the same nationality, Austrian, but replaced Gerhard at Benetton. And it would be a fool who failed to spot that he has the skills to match, and even beat, his compatriot's achievements.

Neat, polite and enthusiastic, Alexander is extremely quick – as he demonstrated in 1997, when he was given a golden chance in the Benetton team as a temporary substitute for Gerhard. Called in for the Canadian Grand Prix, he qualified just three places behind team-mate Jean Alesi and raced strongly, retiring from sixth place mid-race with transmission failure.

What he did in his second race impressed the team even more, for he qualified ahead of Alesi. Although he made a poor start, he sat on Alesi's tail until their pit stops. He then emerged ahead and stayed there until it started to rain, when he fell behind and then spun off. Making up for this error, he sat on Alesi's tail

throughout the British Grand Prix as they raced to places in the top three and, in so doing, he equalled Ralf Schumacher's feat of finishing third in his third Grand Prix. But then Berger returned to the fray having recovered from sinus problems, and Alexander slipped back into Benetton's test team, for whom he conducted an enormous number of miles – many of which were at session-topping pace.

Although he seemed to move easily on to the pace of team-mate Giancarlo Fisichella in 1998, he never made it to the podium – despite five times finishing fourth in the first half of the season before the team began to struggle as Williams and Jordan found their feet.

A family hobby

Alexander's family loves motor racing, as his grandfather used to compete and his father was a rallycross star in the 1970s. However, Alexander has an unusual background in that he cut his teeth in BMX cycle-racing events rather than karting. In fact, he was world champion at

BMX. But as soon as he came of age it was time to go car racing, and Alexander made an impact in Formula Ford in 1992, winning the German and Austrian titles. Three seasons of Formula Three followed, and Alexander won the Austrian series in 1993, was runner-up in the German series in 1994, but took a backward step to be sixth in 1995. However, he landed a drive with Opel in the International Touring Car series in 1996, even taking time out to win the Le Mans 24 Hours race. And he maintained his sports-car connections by being a race-winning member of the Mercedes GT team in 1997.

ONE DAY ALEX... Success is sure to follow for Wurz, even if it didn't come his way in 1998

SAUBER

PROGRESS ESSENTIAL

Sauber failed to move up a gear in 1998, despite having Ferrari engines and two good drivers. So the pressure is on to make progress this year, with Pedro Diniz joining Jean Alesi.

THE VIPs

Peter Sauber

Former sportscar racer who moved to become a constructor. The success of his cars led to Mercedes making Sauber its racing department in 1988, wiping up in sportscars in 1989 by winning both the title and the Le Mans 24 Hours. Won title again in 1990. Entered Formula One in 1993, but lost Mercedes support at end of 1994.

Osamu Goto

The brain behind Honda's ultra-successful involvement in Formula One through the 1980s, Goto moved from Honda to McLaren in 1991 and then on to Ferrari to run its engine programme in 1994. Became head of Sauber's engine department when it took Petronas-badged Ferrari engines in 1997.

STILL LOOKING: Peter Sauber is still on the lookout for his team's first Formula One victory

There's something about Sauber that suggests that it will never really cut it in Formula One. Maybe it's the fact that Switzerland has no racing history. Maybe it's the fact that Switzerland, unlike England, has no motorsport industry infrastructure. Or maybe it's the fact that a cuckoo clock is its chosen timepiece rather than, say, the Tag-Heuer watch associated with McLaren.

Or, maybe it's just that it has an adequate budget from Red Bull and from the Malaysian Petronas group, but not enough to perform the regular testing that increasingly proves the difference between snapping at the heels of the leading group or languishing in the nether reaches of the midfield.

Sauber had two main challenges in 1998. Firstly, it had to continue to push for its first win. And, secondly, it had to prove that it could run two cars to the same level so that it could start gathering regular points towards its tally in the Constructors' Cup, a measure of the real worth of a team.

In Jean Alesi and Johnny Herbert, the Swiss team had two Grand Prix winners. Thanks to their experience – and they had an awful lot for a combined tally of just three wins – they were the sorts of driver who would score whenever the car was up to it. But last year that wasn't very often at all, with Herbert claiming only one point for sixth in the first race and then no more, with just about every sort of car failure imaginable afflicting him, including spinning off in the Italian Grand Prix at Monza as a mechanic had left a pair of pliers in his footwell. Now that wouldn't happen at McLaren.

Alesi fared better as he assumed the mantle of team leader, scoring on four occasions, with a surprise third place at the Belgian Grand Prix his best result. His fifth place in the next race, the Italian Grand Prix, was also pleasing as this came in a race that hadn't seen such a decimation of the field.

The year ahead

Alesi is staying for a second season, being joined by Pedro Diniz now that Herbert has left for Stewart. Diniz is not expected to take over the role of team leader, but he is no longer the definite number two that he was in his first few years in Formula One. Certainly, he brings a healthy budget, but his on-track performances

in 1997 when he sometimes outraced Damon Hill at Arrows, and then when he was joined at Arrows by Mika Salo last year, show that he's made impressive progress.

For the team to make progress as a whole, it must start testing more. Secondly, Sauber must start to operate as a serious team, as one dreads to think of the tantrum Alesi would throw were he to retire due to an errant pair of pliers...

After two years of technical support from Ferrari, Sauber will have to go it alone with its Ferrari-derived Petronas engines in 1999.

Sportscar glory

Sauber burst into Formula One in 1993 after an illustrious career in sportscar racing, winning both the Le Mans 24 Hours and the World Sportscar Championship for Mercedes in 1989. It scored on its debut, thanks to JJ Lehto finishing fifth in the South African Grand Prix. He and Karl Wendlinger then collected a fourth place apiece, but Lehto was replaced in 1994 by Heinz-Harald Frentzen, who was to remain a favourite until he joined Williams in 1997, with third place in the 1995 Italian Grand Prix – his greatest result.

The team was struck a cruel blow in 1994, though, when Wendlinger crashed at Monaco and was left in a coma for three weeks. Although he recovered and Sauber let him race before the end of the year, he was never the same again. Persevering with Ford power in 1996, Frentzen was joined by Herbert, who he outscored, but Herbert produced the best result with third at Monaco.

Ferrari power was harnessed for 1997 and it showed immediate promise, but Herbert was knocked out of the first race at the first corner in the same accident as pole-sitter Jacques Villeneuve. Luckily, team-mate Nicola Larini finished sixth on his Formula One return. Larini's form was to disappoint, and he was replaced by Gianni Morbidelli, who fared better but crashed and broke an arm, forcing him to miss three races. He shunted again in Japan and was again replaced by Norberto Fontana. Herbert, though, was rewarded with third in the Hungarian Grand Prix.

FOR THE RECORD

Country of origin:	Switzerland
Team base:	Hinwil, Switzerland
Founded:	1970
Active in Formula One:	From 1993
Grands Prix contested:	97
Grand Prix wins:	None
Pole positions:	None
Fastest laps:	None

Drivers and Results 1998

Driver	Nationality	Races	Wins	Pts	Pos
Jean Alesi	French	16	0	9	11th
Johnny Herbert	English	16	0	1	15th=

Car specifications

Sponsors:	Petronas and Red Bull
Team principals:	Peter Sauber
Team manager:	Beat Zehnder
Designer:	Leo Ress
Chief engineer:	Ernst Keller
Drivers:	Jean Alesi and Pedro Diniz
Test driver:	tba
Chassis:	Sauber C18
Engine:	Petronas V10
Tyres:	Bridgestone

JEAN ALESI

STILL IN LOVE WITH RACING

Jean Alesi proved with Sauber in 1998 that he's still in love with racing, giving his all with an uncompetitive car. Expect more of the same this season, especially in wet conditions.

MR EXPERIENCE: Jean Alesi – onetime hot-headed novice – is the longest-serving of today's Formula One drivers. And one of the fastest

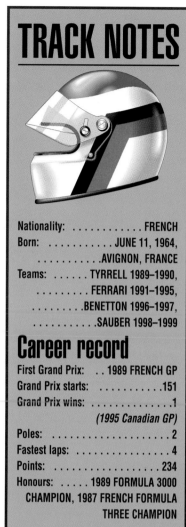

TRACK NOTES

Nationality: . . . . FRENCH
Born: . . . . JUNE 11, 1964,
. . . . .AVIGNON, FRANCE
Teams: . . . . . . TYRRELL 1989–1990,
. . . . FERRARI 1991–1995,
. . . . .BENETTON 1996–1997,
. . . . .SAUBER 1998–1999

Career record

First Grand Prix: . . 1989 FRENCH GP
Grand Prix starts: 151
Grand Prix wins: 1
(1995 Canadian GP)
Poles: 2
Fastest laps: 4
Points: 234
Honours: . . . . . 1989 FORMULA 3000
CHAMPION, 1987 FRENCH FORMULA
THREE CHAMPION

Jean Alesi is a racer of the old school. He cares little for professionalism and the politically correct approach of the modern age: he simply wants a racing car and, if possible, a wet track. Yes, he's a racer through and through.

The popular image of Jean and the reality don't always sit easily together. Think of Alesi and you conjure up the image of a brooding Frenchman with a flash temper and the ability to shine in the most flamboyant way possible – a flawed genius prone to mistakes. While this is based on truth, the reality is more staid, as Alesi is currently the most experienced driver in Formula One, a driver who can be trusted to bring the car home in the points. Except on that

rare occasion in Melbourne in 1997 when he ignored all messages from the pits, his pit board and the evidence that his rivals were making pit stops, and carried on until he ran out of fuel... Yet, amazingly, he has scored just one win in his 151 Grand Prix starts, a figure that is well short of what people expected from someone who was fourth on his Formula One debut.

His move to Sauber last year was seen as a strange one, quitting Benetton – a team that has plenty of wins to its credit – for one that has none. Yet, there was more to it than met the eye. Firstly, it had been made clear to him early last season that Benetton team boss Flavio Briatore didn't want him around, especially after that

incident in Australia. Secondly, Sauber uses Petronas engines, which are rebadged Ferraris, and Jean raced for the Italian team for five seasons from 1991, scoring his lone win for Ferrari in Canada in 1995. Thirdly, he signed a two-year contract that not only meant he will be in Formula One until the end of 1999, but also that he'd be able to gather a huge nest-egg for his retirement.

Jean failed to get on with team-mate Johnny Herbert last year at Sauber, with the English driver soon realizing that the Frenchman had team boss Peter Sauber's ear and that he'd been pushed to the sidelines.

But while Herbert had endless trouble finishing races, frequently retiring with mechanical problems, Jean scored four times, peaking with third place at the accident-strewn Belgian Grand Prix. He also just missed giving Sauber its first pole position at the Austrian Grand Prix when he was pipped by Giancarlo Fisichella's Benetton – the last car to take the flag on a drying track. Indeed, Jean is challenged only by Michael Schumacher when the rain comes down, and he's a joy to watch. He's bound to shine again in 1999.

PEDRO DINIZ

THE MAN ON THE MOVE

TRACK NOTES

Nationality: . . . . BRAZILIAN
Born: . . . . MAY 22, 1970,
. . . . .SAO PAULO, BRAZIL
Teams: . . . . . . FORTI CORSE 1995,
. . . . LIGIER 1996,
. . . . ARROWS 1997, 1998
. . . . .SAUBER 1999

Career record

First Grand Prix: . 1995 BRAZILIAN GP
Grand Prix starts: 66
Grand Prix wins: . . . . NONE
*(best result: fifth in the 1997
Luxembourg GP and 1998 Belgian GP)*
Poles: . . . . NONE
Fastest laps: . . . . NONE
Points: 7
Honours: . . . . NONE

Pedro's move to Sauber will take him to his fourth team in five years. But, at last, he is being signed for his skills as well as for his vast wealth. Whether he can match Jean Alesi is another question. But watch with interest.

It has taken Pedro Diniz four years in Formula One to shake off his tag of being a "rentadriver". Now, after campaigns with Forti, Ligier and Arrows, he is accepted as a driver with or without his bulging briefcase full of money.

Last year was spent alongside the highly rated Mika Salo at Arrows. And, as when he partnered reigning World Champion Damon Hill

year when he was displaced as Sauber's favourite by Jean Alesi. But Pedro will have to outperform his more illustrious team-mate Alesi to achieve the number-one status.

Pedro will be anxious not to experience last year's disappointments again, as team owner Tom Walkinshaw's bold plans failed to hit the target, save for at Monaco where Salo and Diniz were fourth and sixth, and then at Spa where

WATCHING AND WAITING: Pedro Diniz is getting ever closer to producing a drive that will see him on the podium. Maybe it will happen with Sauber?

at the same team in 1997, he wasn't overawed. Yet, unhappy with progress at Arrows, he has joined Sauber – a team that scored few more points than his former team in 1998. However, Pedro is attracted by its Petronas-badged Ferrari engines, units that offered far more power than Arrows' own.

A big question will be how he is welcomed by a team that is not known for providing equal treatment, as Johnny Herbert found out last

Pedro salvaged fifth place from a race of attrition.

Sadly, all too often the Arrows would pull off with mechanical failure, especially as the team introduced engines of yet more advanced specification. The drivers were frustrated, as they felt the John Barnard-designed chassis was a good one, but it was also let down by the Bridgestone tyres that were increasingly disappointing to all of their users bar McLaren, around whose requirements they were

developed as the season progressed.

Cash before talent

Pedro raced karts. Then, encouraged by his father – who had also been a racer – he tried Formula Ford. This was followed in 1990 by a largely fruitless season in Formula Three, before heading to the British series in 1991, driving for the crack West Surrey Racing alongside Rubens Barrichello. Pedro moved to Edenbridge Racing in 1992 and collected two third places. He then spent two years with the Forti Corse Formula 3000 team, peaking with fourth at Estoril in 1994 before graduating to Formula One with Forti in 1995. But the team was miles off the pace, and he struggled.

In 1996 he moved to Ligier, where people failed to notice his progress. He even outqualified team-mate Panis for the French Grand Prix, and ran ahead of him until retiring. That Pedro's first point came in the 1996 Spanish Grand Prix is proof of how many drivers fell off the circuit in the torrential conditions, but Pedro didn't. Then in 1997 he scored but once for Arrows, with fifth place at the Luxembourg Grand Prix, although occasionally outracing his illustrious team-mate, Damon Hill.

ARROWS

PROGRESS NEEDED

Arrows was the disappointment of the 1998 season, when it failed to make the most of its excellent chassis. Now it's lost Pedro Diniz's much-needed finance as well, but it has a new owner in reborn Formula One team Zakspeed.

A TROUBLED YEAR: Arrows boss Tom Walkinshaw was not seen to smile very often in the 1998 season

THE VIPs

Tom Walkinshaw
Tough ex-racer who takes no prisoners and gets what he wants. Formed Tom Walkinshaw Racing in 1976 and has since run works touring-car teams for Mazda, Jaguar, Holden and Volvo. Brought Jaguar great success in sportscars before moving into Formula One with Benetton. Masterminded Michael Schumacher's 1994 title, then took over Ligier before buying Arrows.

Peter Zakowski
A former Formula Three racer, Peter is the 32-year-old son of former Zakspeed Formula One team entrant Erich Zakowski and has been in charge of the family team for several years, most recently running a pair of Porsches in the FIA GT Championship.

thumb his nose at Frank Williams for showing him the door. Others felt a win was possible as a precursor to greater things in 1998. Yet they were all wrong.

For the record, Hill did not challenge for the title in 1997 before moving on to Jordan for last season. In fact, he didn't even win a race, although he came within half a lap of winning the Hungarian GP before being demoted to second by eventual champion Jacques Villeneuve's Williams. Contemporary Formula One is just too tough for a team to turn around and topple the major teams. But the foundations were laid for greater things, with the arrival of the much-feted designer John Barnard expected to help improve matters.

A year of woe

Pedro Diniz had gone a good way towards shaking off his tag of being simply a rentadriver in 1997, when he even outraced Hill on several occasions, but for 1998 he was expected to have to prove himself all over again with the arrival of the highly-rated Mika Salo from Tyrrell. To the casual spectator, this was seen as a backward step, as Arrows was filling the shoes of a driver who scored seven points in 1997 with one who took home two. But a close look at the earlier stages of his career reveals that Salo pushed compatriot Mika Hakkinen hard for the British Formula Three crown back in 1990. And so the battle began, with Salo coming out ahead.

However, both drivers suffered from two major failings: the cars were underpowered due to weak engines; and secondly they suffered numerous mechanical failures. The Barnard-designed chassis looked magnificent in their predominantly black livery, but however good they were they simply lacked the horsepower to show their merits. Certainly, the Arrows-badged engines turned out increasing amounts of horsepower as ever more evolutions were introduced, but it was never enough. Their parlous finishing record meant that the first time an Arrows reached the finish was when Salo

T here has been a great deal of change at Arrows over the close-season, with the ownership of the team being a subject of great debate. For a while it looked as though a Nigerian prince would be taking control from Tom Walkinshaw. But, at the time of writing, a deal is being cemented for former Formula One team Zakspeed to take the reins with backing from the district of Germany from which it operates.

An improvement in form is long overdue, especially as some of the tabloid newspaper writers predicted that Arrows would start winning as soon as reigning World Champion Damon Hill joined team owner Tom Walkinshaw in 1997. Yet, two years on, that elusive first win seems little closer. Arrows had never won before, but with Hill on board and with Walkinshaw's record of winning in whatever he does, the press predicted that results would follow. The more trigger-happy predicted that Hill would be able to score a handful of wins and challenge for the title, and thus

FOR THE RECORD

Country of origin:	England
Team base:	Witney, England
Founded:	1977
Active in Formula One:	From 1978
Grands Prix contested:	321
Grand Prix wins:	None
Pole positions:	None
Fastest laps:	None

Drivers and Results 1998

Driver	Nationality	Races	Wins	Pts	Pos
Pedro Diniz	Brazilian	16	0	3	13th
Mika Salo	Finnish	16	0	3	13th

Car specifications

Sponsors:	Danka, Parmalat, Zepter
Team principals:	Tom Walkinshaw & Peter Zakowski
Team manager:	John Walton
Designer:	Nick Wirth
Chief engineer:	Chris Dyer
Drivers:	Mika Salo and Toranosuke Takagi
Test driver:	tba
Chassis:	Arrows A19
Engine:	Arrows V10
Tyres:	Bridgestone

was ninth in the fourth round, the San Marino GP. Diniz didn't even finish a race until the sixth round at Monaco, when he survived a last-lap assault from Michael Schumacher to claim sixth place. The day was a double success for Arrows as Salo finished fourth.

While this was enormously encouraging, it proved that the cars were effective on a circuit at which ultimate horsepower was not the be-all and end-all. Sadly for Diniz and Salo, it was the only such circuit on the calendar, and they didn't score again until the Belgian GP.

There was another problem: Barnard had used expensive materials in the construction of the chassis, and it cost a bomb when they were wrecked. Thus the Belgian GP marked a very dark weekend for a team that was already known to be not in the best of financial health, when Salo wrote off his car in untimed practice with an enormous accident at Eau Rouge. The bill multiplied the following day when both Arrows were involved in the first lap pile-up. Diniz went some way towards staving off total disaster, though, by taking the spare chassis to fifth place. Salo and Diniz soldiered on, but their best efforts seldom left them ahead of anything other than the Minardis, the Tyrrells and the Stewarts.

The year ahead

Arrows enters 1999 still winless after 321 attempts. And it looks extremely unlikely that the team will make much progress in the season ahead, as not only has its budget been dented by Diniz's decision to quit the team, but Barnard has also left for pastures new, joining up with his former charge, Alain Prost. Salo, too, was looking for a way out as last season drew to a close, but he was contractually obliged to stay on, and must hope that the team can turn the corner before his reputation is dented further by another year in which he has no chance to show his skills.

The second seat has been filled by Toranosuke Takagi, a driver who displayed enormous natural speed – if little discipline – in his rookie season with Tyrrell. If Walkinshaw can control this quiet Japanese driver and bring the best out of him, then we may really see something. He could well bring the best out of Salo by putting him under pressure in qualifying.

> **THE MONEY MAN: Pedro Diniz will be missed in 1999, and not only because he won't be bringing a budget**

MIKA SALO

MARKING TIME

Is Mika Salo as quick as his World Champion Finnish contemporary Mika Hakkinen? We will never know until he lands a drive with a more competitive team than Arrows.

A FRUSTRATED TALENT: Mika Salo has the skills to shine, but has never had the right machinery

TRACK NOTES

Nationality: . . . . FINNISH
Born: . . . . . . NOVEMBER 30, 1966,
. . . . HELSINKI, FINLAND
Teams: . . . . LOTUS 1994,
. . . . TYRRELL 1995–1997,
. . . . ARROWS 1998–1999

Career record

First Grand Prix: . 1994 JAPANESE GP
Grand Prix starts: 68
Grand Prix wins: . . . . NONE
    (best result: fourth, 1998 Monaco GP)
Poles: . . . . NONE
Fastest laps: . . . . NONE
Points: 15
Honours: . . 1990 BRITISH FORMULA
THREE RUNNER-UP, 1988 EUROPEAN
FORMULA FORD CHAMPION

The parallels between Mika Salo and Mika Hakkinen are far greater than people would have realized at Suzuka last November, when the former struggled at the rear of the field in his Arrows and the latter won in his McLaren to become World Champion. Yes, they are both from Helsinki. Yes, they both fought for the British Formula Three crown in 1990, with Hakkinen easing ahead late in the season. And, yes, they both made it to Formula One without the benefit of substantial sponsorship.

However, only those who scrutinize Formula One will have noticed what Salo has got up to since he graduated from Japanese Formula 3000 at the end of 1994. That's because he has been racing his heart out for teams that are never going to run at the front and are thus ignored by the TV directors. Yet he has been taking his cars to the best result of which they are capable. Sadly, that was only once in the points for Tyrrell in 1997, when he finished fifth in the streaming conditions at Monaco. But like team-mate Jos Verstappen – a driver who was twice third in his rookie year with Benetton – he had to watch those with better cars and better engines claim the points. Salo outqualified Verstappen 10 times in the 17 races, but outraced him in almost every outing. That's why Tom Walkinshaw snapped him up to replace Damon Hill for 1998.

However, Arrows failed to produce a competitive package, as its chassis was compromised by weak engines. Monaco was again Salo's best result as he raced to fourth.

Salo may share a Christian name with Hakkinen, but ask either of them about their relationship, and that's clearly all they share. For these Finns are not the best of friends, and it

goes back a very long way. Following a year behind Hakkinen, Salo won the European Formula Ford title ahead of Michael Schumacher in 1988 before joining Hakkinen in British Formula Three. They fought a season-long battle for the same championship in 1990. Hakkinen won the title and leapt to Formula One, but Salo lacked a budget for Formula 3000 and headed for Japan. Yet all the top Formula 3000 teams there were full, and it took several years to find a competitive drive.

A flying start

Mika's arrival in Formula One caused people to sit up, as Mika did a great job for the dying Lotus team at the end of 1994. Then he ran third in the first Grand Prix of 1995, in Brazil, before suffering cramp that forced him to drive one-handed and eventually spin back to seventh. And this was in a Tyrrell, a car more usually found mid-order.

Despite this impressive start, Mika scored on only three occasions in 1995, while experienced team-mate Ukyo Katayama failed to score even once. The Tyrrell was better in 1996, but all too often they pulled off with engine failures, and 1997 showed little progress.

TORANOSUKE TAKAGI

JAPAN EXPECTS

Toranosuke Takagi excited and disappointed in equal measure in his rookie season with Tyrrell in 1998. While he's quick, he will have to be less wild to improve with Arrows this year.

The Japanese race fan is patient and loyal, ever happy to take a foreign driver to their heart, with Mika Hakkinen (and Ayrton Senna before him) their favourites. However, they would love a driver of their own to star on Formula One's big stage. And they hope that Toranosuke Takagi will become that man. After his first full season in Formula One, though, "Tora" has proved fast but flawed.

Tora would frequently display great speed in his Tyrrell, a car little fancied next to the might of McLaren, Ferrari and the other top teams. But all too often this was in the untimed practice sessions that counted for naught, or in the race-morning warm-up, running in the top half-dozen as he lapped on a light fuel load while the others were out on full tanks. On an equal number of occasions, however, he would slam the car into the barriers, sending team boss Harvey Postlethwaite into orbit as he'd invariably have just asked Tora to do a few careful laps...

Outrunning team-mate Ricardo Rosset, his best result was ninth at the British GP, with a similar position coming his way late in the year in the Italian Grand Prix.

Helped by Nakajima

Tora starred from karting all the way up to Formula Nippon – Japan's version of Formula 3000 (Formula One's international feeder category). From 1994 on, he drove for the Nakajima Planning team, as the *protegé* of former Lotus and Tyrrell driver Satoru Nakajima, pitting himself favourably against the likes of overseas drivers Ralf Schumacher and Norberto Fontana. It should also be noted that he outscored compatriot Shinji Nakano in the two years during which they raced together.

Tora's fame in Japan is greater than almost any of Britain's Formula One drivers receive in Britain, such is the country's fanaticism. That he is seen as a fashion icon, too, doesn't hinder his cause. And, after spending 1997 as Tyrrell's test driver, getting in valuable mileage out of the public eye, he graduated to the British team's race line-up.

Indeed, Nakajima – who had a share-holding in Tyrrell, bringing much-needed backing from the PIAA automotive aftermarket product group – not only made sure that Tora had a deal to test for the team throughout 1997, but he also sorted him a ride in the Porsche Supercup so that he could learn the European circuits used by the Formula One circus. That all 10 of these Supercup races supported Grands Prix was an added bonus, keeping him in with the right crowd. The fact that Tora never finished higher than tenth was of little consequence, as the cars require a particular driving style that many single-seater drivers take time to master.

TRACK NOTES

Nationality: .... JAPANESE
Born: .... FEBRUARY 12, 1974,
.... SHIZUOKA, JAPAN
Teams: .... TYRRELL 1998,
.... ARROWS 1999

Career record

First Grand Prix: 1998 AUSTRALIAN GP
Grand Prix starts: 16
Grand Prix wins: .... NONE
(best result: ninth in the 1998
British GP and 1998 Italian GP)
Poles: .... NONE
Fastest laps: .... NONE
Points: .... NONE
Honours: . 1995 JAPANESE FORMULA
3000 RUNNER-UP, 1994 FIFTH IN
JAPANESE FORMULA THREE, 1990
JAPANESE A2 KART CHAMPION

HAIR-RAISING TALENT: Toranosuke Takagi showed in his rookie Formula One season that he has the speed if not the control required to succeed at this level

STEWART

THIRD TIME LUCKY?

The pressure is on the Stewart team after a disappointing second year in Formula One. This year it must deliver for engine supplier Ford, with new signing Johnny Herbert bringing welcome experience to the mix.

THE VIPs

Jackie Stewart

Three-times World Champion who has shunned thoughts of retirement and formed his own Formula One team. Made Formula One debut with BRM in 1965, scoring the first of his 27 wins that year. Retired from driving in 1973 when team-mate François Cevert was killed. Has since been a commentator and a hugely successful businessman.

Gary Anderson

Ulsterman Gary has a wealth of experience that started when he worked for Brabham and McLaren before forming his own company – Anson – to construct Formula Three and Formula Super Vee chassis. A spell in Indycars was followed by joining Reynard and then being in at the formation of Jordan as the chief designer until he left last year.

Three-times World Champion Jackie Stewart was typically cautious when he announced that he and son Paul were starting a Formula One team for 1997; he reckoned it would be a five-year project to see them challenge for World Championship honours. Onlookers reckoned that with works Ford engines and the quality of personnel he'd assembled around him that this was being very conservative, and that maybe race wins in the second year would be followed by a title bid in 1999. Well, sadly for Jackie, he appears to have been right, and the onlookers can only shuffle off and learn to understand that Formula One is a harder nut to crack than even they thought. For, as fans saw last year, Stewart is still a long way from glory, fighting as it is to secure its place in the midfield.

It is often said that a team's second season is harder than the first, as team personnel were too busy working on getting the first year's car to work to concentrate on developing the car for the second year. However, there was more to Stewart's thin time in 1998, such as too many mechanical failures. Just ask the drivers: Rubens Barrichello, Jan Magnussen and Jos Verstappen. Yes, there were three last year, as Magnussen was kicked out after the Canadian Grand Prix where, ironically, he had scored a valuable point for sixth place. In came Verstappen, being given yet another chance to get his foot in Formula One's door. However, the Dutchman failed to do any better than the Dane, also lagging behind the Brazilian team leader. But rare was the day that both Stewarts finished, so if the team is to be more of a factor in the year ahead, reliability must be sorted.

The end-of-year tally of five points for Barrichello's fifth-place finishes

IN FROM THE BEGINNING: Rubens Barrichello has been the backbone of the Stewart team's driving line-up since 1997, but is now impatient for results

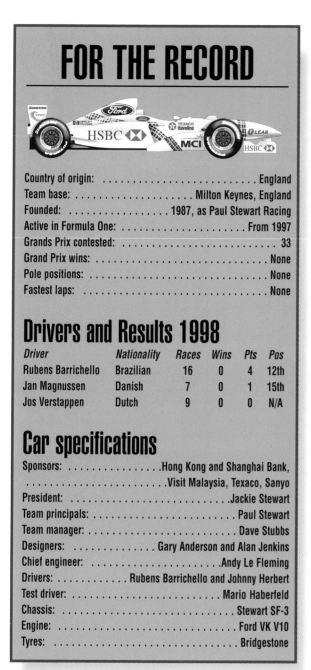

FOR THE RECORD

Country of origin:	England
Team base:	Milton Keynes, England
Founded:	1987, as Paul Stewart Racing
Active in Formula One:	From 1997
Grands Prix contested:	33
Grand Prix wins:	None
Pole positions:	None
Fastest laps:	None

Drivers and Results 1998

Driver	Nationality	Races	Wins	Pts	Pos
Rubens Barrichello	Brazilian	16	0	4	12th
Jan Magnussen	Danish	7	0	1	15th
Jos Verstappen	Dutch	9	0	0	N/A

Car specifications

Sponsors:	Hong Kong and Shanghai Bank, Visit Malaysia, Texaco, Sanyo
President:	Jackie Stewart
Team principals:	Paul Stewart
Team manager:	Dave Stubbs
Designers:	Gary Anderson and Alan Jenkins
Chief engineer:	Andy Le Fleming
Drivers:	Rubens Barrichello and Johnny Herbert
Test driver:	Mario Haberfeld
Chassis:	Stewart SF-3
Engine:	Ford VK V10
Tyres:	Bridgestone

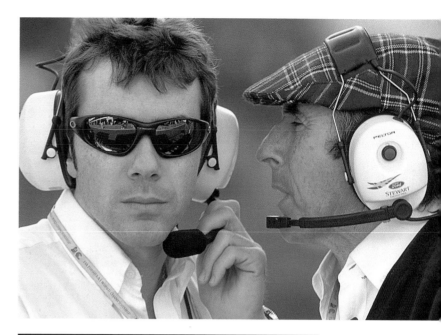

in the Spanish and Canadian Grands Prix and Magnussen's sixth place in Canada didn't leave Stewart as the worst team, but there is ample scope for improvement, and all involved will be praying for an effective chassis from the design department now that the team has poached Gary Anderson from Jordan, with the Ulsterman bringing a wealth of experience to work in conjunction with Alan Jenkins. Add to this a stronger Ford engine – which is sure to happen now that Ford owns engine-builder Cosworth, rather than simply contracting it to build its racing engines, as it has in the past – and you can see why Stewart's form should improve in 1999.

A proven race winner

A trump card for the season ahead, however, is the signing of Johnny Herbert to partner Barrichello. Yes, Stewart has long expounded the promotion of young talent. But that didn't work with Magnussen, and in Herbert he has a driver who not only brings huge experience, but knows how to win, having done so twice for Benetton in 1995.

The Stewart team's two-year history should not be seen only in terms of failure, more as a case of failing to achieve the expectations of others. And one day stands out above all others, this coming at the Monaco Grand Prix in 1997 when Jackie and son Paul were ecstatic when Barrichello finished second after a sensible and skilled drive in the rain. Jackie was even moved to say he'd never felt so emotional about racing, not even when driving. That's quite something from a man who won three World Championships. However, that remained the highlight, and no more points followed for either him or for Magnussen – both seen all too often pulling off after yet another engine blow-up. Indeed, between them they reached the finish just six times out of a possible total of 34. Mind you, as the men at Ford fought their way through 1997 and found more power from their engine, progress was made up the grid, with the drivers sharing the third row for the Austrian Grand Prix. Typically, though, the cars were both parked up before the race was over.

Last year saw no such high points, although Barrichello frequently shone if the track was damp or fully wet, showing that his once widely acknowledged skills were still present. Magnussen knew from early in the season that he was under inspection, with Jackie and Paul still not sure that the laid-back Dane was applying himself fully. They made the hard decision to drop him before the French Grand Prix. Still, they gave him a season and a half to make a go of things. For those who saw him clean up in British Formula Three, he proved to be an enigma. But maybe he didn't really want it enough, or simply suffered from being number two in a team that struggled to provide a reliable package even for its number one driver. After all, a driver doesn't forget how to drive overnight...

Keeping up appearances

Renowned for their meticulous approach, the Stewart team was immediately one of the slickest in the paddock, impressing all with its appearance, even though some railed at the sight of Stewart *pere et fils* sporting their "Racing Stewart" tartan trews and matching caps. But no one expected anything less than this first class level of professionalism, as Jackie Stewart was effectively the first professional Formula One driver. Not because he was the first to be paid for his services, but because he was the first to embrace practices and principles that we see today as being "professional".

RUBENS BARRICHELLO

TIME TO DELIVER

Rubens Barrichello had hoped that Stewart would make progress in 1998. It didn't and he wanted to move elsewhere. But he failed to find a way out, and must dig deep for his motivation in his third year with the team.

Rubens Barrichello has yet to make the impression on Formula One that his skills suggest. For, after 97 Grands Prix, he is still without a victory, and this is not what you would have predicted if you'd seen him shoot through the junior categories to become a Grand Prix driver before his 21st birthday.

Ultra-quick in karts, Rubens moved to Formula Ford and attracted a consortium of businessmen who offered to take him to Europe, and hopefully all the way to Formula One. Only then would they want anything in return. Freed from financial worries, Rubens won the European Formula Opel series in 1990 and then the 1991 British Formula Three Championship. After a mixed season in Formula 3000 in 1992, he joined Jordan and astonished everyone by running second to Ayrton Senna in the wet at Donington Park in only his third Grand Prix. But the next three years at Jordan were largely fruitless except for second place in Canada in 1995. By the end of 1996, people were saying that he'd lost his edge and was considering a move to Indycars. But then former World Champion Jackie Stewart signed the mercurial Brazilian for the Stewart team.

Life at Stewart

By scoring only six points in 1997, he was eight points down on the 1996 tally that cost him his ride at Jordan, but the fact that Rubens finished just twice in 17 starts wasn't his fault, as Stewart suffered endless new-team problems – the majority of which were engine failures. Yet Rubens was happier than he'd been for years, for he was made to feel wanted. What's more, there was evident promise as the team – and particularly its explosive Ford engines – became ever more competitive, to the extent that he and team-mate Jan Magnussen qualified fifth and sixth, respectively, for the Austrian Grand Prix. Again he retired, but this time it was his fault, sliding off when pressured by a recovering Michael Schumacher. But the highlight was his second place in very wet conditions at Monaco, where he outraced all his rivals except Schumacher, triggering tears of joy in the Stewart camp.

Sadly, 1998 saw no progress and, with the exception of a pair of fifth-place finishes in Spain and Canada, the car seldom finished. The only chance Rubens had to show his skill was whenever the circuit was wet, in which conditions he was invariably one of the fastest.

Looking for a more competitive ride for 1999, Rubens talked to Williams, but he couldn't afford to buy himself out of his contract, so he's staying on for a third season.

TRACK NOTES

Nationality: . . . . BRAZILIAN
Born: . . . . MAY 23, 1972,
. . . . .SAO PAULO, BRAZIL
Teams: . . . . . . JORDAN 1993–1996,
. . . . STEWART 1997–1999

Career record
First Grand Prix: 1993
. . . . .SOUTH AFRICAN GP
Grand Prix starts: 97
Grand Prix wins: . . . . NONE
(best result: second,
1995 Canadian GP,
1997 Monaco GP)
Poles: 1
Fastest laps: . . . . NONE
Points: 56
Honours: . . 1991 BRITISH FORMULA
THREE CHAMPION, 1990 GM
EUROSERIES CHAMPION, 1988
BRAZILIAN KARTING CHAMPION

STILL SMILING: Barrichello won't be if his results don't improve

JOHNNY HERBERT

A NEW CHALLENGE

Johnny Herbert fell out of favour at Sauber last year and is now faced with the challenge of propelling Stewart up the grid. His Grand Prix-winning experience and speed could really help the team hit the big time.

THE FACE OF EXPERIENCE: Johnny Herbert knows what it takes to win

TRACK NOTES

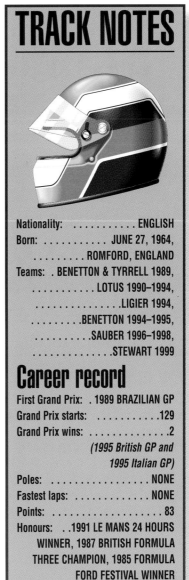

Nationality:	ENGLISH
Born:	JUNE 27, 1964,
	ROMFORD, ENGLAND
Teams:	BENETTON & TYRRELL 1989,
	LOTUS 1990–1994,
	LIGIER 1994,
	BENETTON 1994–1995,
	SAUBER 1996–1998,
	STEWART 1999

Career record
First Grand Prix:	1989 BRAZILIAN GP
Grand Prix starts:	129
Grand Prix wins:	2
	(1995 British GP and 1995 Italian GP)
Poles:	NONE
Fastest laps:	NONE
Points:	83
Honours:	1991 LE MANS 24 HOURS WINNER, 1987 BRITISH FORMULA THREE CHAMPION, 1985 FORMULA FORD FESTIVAL WINNER

Few drivers have more cause than Johnny Herbert to wonder how their Formula One career went off the rails. For he arrived with all the promise in the world in 1989, and a decade later is still fighting for the respect he deserves.

After a karting career that included two British titles, Johnny won the 1985 Formula Ford Festival. He then lifted the British Formula Three title for Eddie Jordan in 1987 and won first time out in Formula 3000. But his year was cut short by a violent accident at Brands Hatch that left him with serious foot injuries. Ironically, that very morning he had signed to drive for Benetton for 1989. After a winter of physiotherapy, Johnny finished fourth first time out in Brazil, just ten seconds behind race-winner Nigel Mansell. However, it soon

became clear that his injuries were not fully healed and he was dropped. Occasional drives with Tyrrell and Lotus and a season in Japanese Formula 3000 followed, but Lotus picked him up full-time for 1991 and his career was back on track, although the team was on its last legs.

Life at Benetton in 1995 saw him challenge team-mate Michael Schumacher at the first race, but then the team concentrated solely on the German and appeared almost not to care that Johnny won the British and Italian Grands Prix, so it was small wonder that he was happy to move to Sauber for 1996.

By 1997, he was team leader at Sauber, taking over once Heinz-Harald Frentzen had left for Williams, and the season looked as though

it would be a good one, as he was one of the front-runners in Australia. Down to the first corner, that is, where he was knocked off the circuit by Jacques Villeneuve, who had been hit by Eddie Irvine. So, no points, and none came his way until Brazil, where Johnny was fourth. A pair of fifths followed, but Johnny peaked with a third place in Hungary, equalling Sauber's best-ever result. However, a lack of testing and development cost dearly, and he was normally just outside the points.

Sixth place in last year's season-opener at Melbourne made it look as though this would be a better season. But this was Johnny's only point all year, and he soon found himself demoted to the team's number-two seat by Jean Alesi – a driver whom they grew to love, even though he knocked Johnny off the circuit on the first lap of an untimed session in Argentina.

However, Stewart made a wise decision in signing Johnny, as he still has the speed and the experience they need to and move up the order.

PROST

TIME TO GET SERIOUS

Alain Prost was a very unhappy man last year as he became fully acquainted with the rigours of running a Formula One team and, even more alien to him, with being an also-ran. Expect a fightback.

A STUDY OF PRECISION: Alain Prost wants the Prost team to run like clockwork in the season ahead

Alain Prost wants one thing above all others in the season ahead: stability, as only when this is in place can his eponymous team make strides towards the front of the grid. His first step towards stability came last August at the Hungarian Grand Prix, when he firmed up his driver line-up for 1999. After some serious talking, Olivier Panis agreed to stay on for his sixth season with the team, with Jarno Trulli putting approaches from the likes of Williams to one side to concentrate on his future with the French team. Panis, it seems, had become disillusioned with the team's direction, and had to be convinced that changes on the

technical side were going to be implemented before he put his name on the dotted line.

In fairness to Panis, this wasn't a case of being petty as a way of deflecting attention from the fact that he had not scored a point, rather a case of wanting things to be better – much better. And he had a point, as Prost had had the first half of its season ruined by endless gearbox problems. So the news that Prost was pushing to recruit former McLaren and Ferrari design chief John Barnard – whom he knows so well from their World Championship-winning time together at McLaren in the 1980s – to

FOR THE RECORD

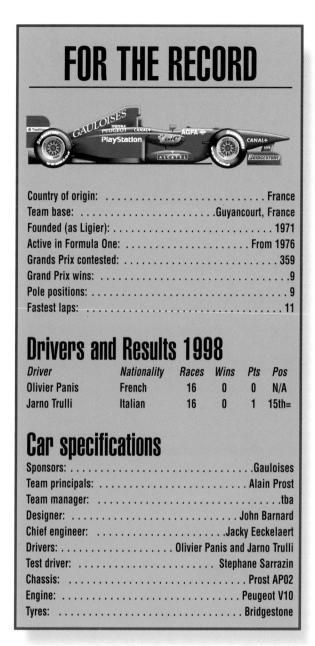

Country of origin:	France
Team base:	Guyancourt, France
Founded (as Ligier):	1971
Active in Formula One:	From 1976
Grands Prix contested:	359
Grand Prix wins:	9
Pole positions:	9
Fastest laps:	11

Drivers and Results 1998

Driver	Nationality	Races	Wins	Pts	Pos
Olivier Panis	French	16	0	0	N/A
Jarno Trulli	Italian	16	0	1	15th=

Car specifications

Sponsors:	Gauloises
Team principals:	Alain Prost
Team manager:	tba
Designer:	John Barnard
Chief engineer:	Jacky Eeckelaert
Drivers:	Olivier Panis and Jarno Trulli
Test driver:	Stephane Sarrazin
Chassis:	Prost AP02
Engine:	Peugeot V10
Tyres:	Bridgestone

ALAIN, I THINK… Jarno Trulli puts his point across to Alain Prost during last year's troubled campaign

retirement after retirement that left Panis with a ninth place in the opening race as his best result. No wonder he was disillusioned, as the year before he had been in the top three twice before breaking his legs. Trulli, on the other hand, was also hit by the same problems, as well as the car's inherent twitchiness on the entry to corners, but held it all together to collect sixth place at the battle-torn Belgian Grand Prix. This was a very important point to gain, as it meant that Prost was able to claim some of the official travel fund for 1999, worth about £1.5 million.

Despite the team saying as early as the Hungarian Grand Prix that it had decided to concentrate on its 1999 car rather than "wasting" undue effort to sort its 1998 offering, the drivers were cheered at the Italian Grand Prix, three races before the end of the season when rear suspension modifications made the first big improvement experienced all year, and both qualified in the top 10. Although this produced no points as they hit assorted problems in the race, Trulli showed flashes of the skill that had seen him lead the Austrian Grand Prix in 1997 when driving as a stand-in for Panis, to set the race's fifth-fastest lap.

Promise rather than results

When Panis scored his surprise victory in the wet at Monaco in 1996, Ligier became a winning team for the first time since Jacques Laffite triumphed in Canada all the way back in 1981, adding to the eight wins that the team scored between 1977 and 1981. So, the history of the team that was transformed into Prost is a long and not always illustrious one.

It's not just its on-track performance that has been chequered. Take, for example, its ownership. Considering Ligier has been in Formula One only since 1976, it has had an extraordinary number of changes of ownership. From former rugby player and occasional 1960s Formula One racer Guy Ligier, it passed on to financier Cyril de Rouvre in 1992 after a take-over bid by Alain Prost had failed. Then de Rouvre was jailed for fraud and the then Benetton boss Flavio Briatore took over in 1994. Tom Walkinshaw grabbed the reins in 1996 and threatened to make the team move to Britain in a quest to make it more competitive. This rocked the French, as it would have left the country that invented motor racing without a team of its own. However, Walkinshaw sold out and went to Arrows, leaving the way clear for Prost to take over.

produce a chassis that would make the most of the ample Peugeot horsepower on tap was just what Olivier wanted to hear. And, clearly, he needs to be fired up to give his all in the season ahead to save his career. Equally, Prost will have to try to convince the extravagant Barnard to keep costs in check, for he is famed for building beautiful and effective chassis – as at Arrows last year – but making them from ultra-expensive material that can take a chunk out of any budget.

This emphasized that while Prost wants the team to win for the glory of France, he is not averse to bringing in foreigners to help them achieve that aim. A British-designed, French-built chassis powered by French engines and driven by one French driver and one Italian isn't that far from the ultimate aim after all. Especially if it turns the team into winners, at which point the non-French elements can be replaced.

A disappointing year

It appeared at the outset of last year that Prost had pulled off a shrewd deal in signing Bernard Dudot to look after the technical side of the programme. But Dudot – a veteran of 20 years with Renault's all-conquering Formula One programme – failed to make the whole package work, and the gearbox was the weak point in the Loic Bigois-designed AP01 chassis, leading to

OLIVIER PANIS

TIME TO DELIVER

This is a make-or-break year for Olivier Panis, as the one-time Grand Prix winner must return to form with the Prost team or risk being replaced in Formula One by the younger hotshots waiting in the wings.

For years, Olivier Panis was seen as the man to take France back to the front in Formula One. Adored for winning in soaking conditions at Monaco in 1996, he led Alain Prost's team through its first season in 1997 and shone. But a poor 1998 season has reduced Olivier to a man on the margins who must bounce back or risk being shown the one-way door out of Formula One.

An ace in karting, Olivier won a Formula Renault scholarship in 1988 and was French champion in 1989. Formula Three also took two attempts, with Olivier being runner-up in 1991. Formula 3000 was his third two-year project, and he won the 1993 title to be shot into Formula One with Ligier. Olivier finished 15 of the 16 Grands Prix in his maiden season, also scoring more points than his experienced team-mate Eric Bernard. He therefore kept the drive for 1995, improving to eighth overall, helped by a surprise second place in the final race in Australia. Despite his Monaco win, however, 1996 was a disappointment.

Olivier's darkest day

However, it's a miracle that Olivier is racing at all, for at Montreal in 1997 his car appeared to suffer suspension failure and was pitched into the barriers, breaking his legs. Astonishingly, he was back racing again for the Luxembourg Grand Prix that September.

Heartening as this was, one had to feel sorry for Olivier as the accident had curtailed a season in which everything seemed to be falling into place, with a good chassis inherited from Ligier, a strong engine from Mugen and durable tyres from Bridgestone. Fifth place in Australia showed promise, third in Brazil made people sit up, then retirement from second place in Argentina proved that success was at hand. But his fourth race, at Imola, proved that Bridgestone could also get it wrong and Olivier struggled home eighth. Fourth place in the wet at Monaco was followed by second in Spain. But then came that race in Canada...

Fully recovered for 1998, it should have come right, especially with lusty Peugeot engines. But the car was hampered by an experimental gearbox, and it wasn't until the thirteenth race that a point was scored. This was courtesy of his team-mate Jarno Trulli, a driver who had taken over as the team's favourite, showing just how disenchanted Olivier had become. Indeed, finishing ninth and last in the opening race in Melbourne was still his best result by the middle of August, when he begrudgingly re-signed for 1999, kept on for a sixth year only when it seemed likely that John Barnard would be joining to head the design team.

TRACK NOTES

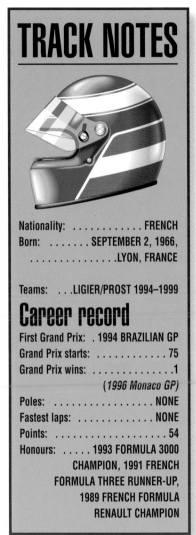

Nationality: . . . . FRENCH
Born: . . . . SEPTEMBER 2, 1966,
. . . . .LYON, FRANCE

Teams: . . .LIGIER/PROST 1994–1999

Career record
First Grand Prix: . 1994 BRAZILIAN GP
Grand Prix starts: 75
Grand Prix wins: 1
(*1996 Monaco GP*)
Poles: . . . . NONE
Fastest laps: . . . . NONE
Points: 54
Honours: . . . . . 1993 FORMULA 3000 CHAMPION, 1991 FRENCH FORMULA THREE RUNNER-UP, 1989 FRENCH FORMULA RENAULT CHAMPION

JARNO TRULLI

POISED TO STRIKE

Jarno Trulli arrived in Formula One with a bang in 1997 and led the Austrian Grand Prix. Last year was a struggle in an uncompetitive Prost car, but he has the makings of being one of the greats. All he needs is the equipment.

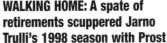

WALKING HOME: A spate of retirements scuppered Jarno Trulli's 1998 season with Prost

Every now and then a driver is seen as the next Stirling Moss, Emerson Fittipaldi or Ayrton Senna, according to the era of their ascendancy. The hotshot bearing these accolades either flowers or wilts under the weight of expectation or from not having the right equipment. And Jarno Trulli is the latest one to watch, having risen to Formula One faster than anyone before. Now under the tutelage of four-times World Champion Alain Prost, this 24-year-old Italian is receiving the very best advice. However, he will only realize the promise of his talents if the team gives him a much better car than last year's.

One of the all-time karting heroes, Jarno was spotted by former Benetton boss Flavio Briatore and propelled directly into Formula Three mid-way through 1995. He learned fast and won the final two races of the German series. Returning in 1996, Jarno won the German title and said that Formula 3000 would be an unnecessary step for him. How right he was...

Jarno finished second to last at his first Grand Prix in Australia, but he was driving a Minardi and could expect little better. He also finished his next two races, and this is all one can ask of a rookie driver, as there is no substitute for race mileage. It was all the more valuable as Jarno had joined the team at the very last minute, and had scarcely sat in the car before Melbourne.

Jarno's lucky break

Jarno was propelled on to a higher plane when Olivier Panis broke his legs in Canada, and he substituted for the Frenchman in the Prost team. Jarno went faster, but he continued to make mistakes that started to annoy Prost. However, all was forgiven in Austria where he qualified third on the grid, got the jump on Michael Schumacher and took the lead when Mika Hakkinen retired on the first lap. Jarno led until his pit stop. Jacques Villeneuve then moved ahead and Jarno was running second in front of David Coulthard when his engine blew. And that was his last race before Panis's return.

Signed as a fully fledged member of the Prost team for 1998, everything was expected to come good, but it never happened. Certainly, Trulli generally outqualified Panis and was the one to break the team's drought, collecting a point for sixth place more through perseverance than speed at the battle-torn Belgian Grand Prix. However, the fact that this was the season's thirteenth race shows how poor Prost's form was; the root cause was the gearbox. Then, by July, Prost admitted that it was concentrating on developing its 1999 car. However, a suspension tweak prior to the Italian Grand Prix helped Jarno to lap fifth quickest in the race, although other problems left him thirteenth and last...

TRACK NOTES

Nationality: . . . . ITALIAN
Born: . . . . JULY 13, 1974,
. . . . PESCARA, ITALY
Teams: . . . . MINARDI 1997,
. . . . PROST 1997–1999

Career record
First Grand Prix: 1997 AUSTRALIAN GP
Grand Prix starts: 30
Grand Prix wins: . . . . NONE
    (best result: fourth, 1997 German GP)
Poles: . . . . NONE
Fastest laps: . . . . NONE
Points: 4
Honours: . . 1996 GERMAN FORMULA
    THREE CHAMPION, 1994 WORLD
    KARTING CHAMPION

MINARDI

STEPPING UP THE PACE

The people behind Minardi have long been seen as happy simply to be in Formula One. Well, that was true, but this year they plan to take a tilt at moving off the back of the grid.

THE VIPs

Giancarlo Minardi
Giancarlo ran a very successful Formula Two team in the late 1970s and early 1980s, then made the jump to Formula One in 1985. It's been tough ever since, with points few and far between, but Giancarlo plugs on, trying out ever more new talent and simply going racing for the love of it.

Gabriele Rumi
Gabriele made his money with the Fondmetal alloy wheels company and has been involved in Formula One since 1984, supplying many teams. He ran his the Fondmetal team between 1990 and 1992, but has since preferred to be involved only as a partner with Minardi – albeit one who is increasingly flexing his muscles in his quest for progress.

BACK FOR MORE: Esteban Tuero arrived at Minardi last year as a teenager and must now put the lessons learned to good effect if he is to help the little Italian team make progress towards the midfield

For far too long, people have looked at Giancarlo Minardi and said that there's something lovable about the way in which he and his little team of Italians go about their business in Formula One. In a patronizing fashion, even insiders have celebrated the wonderful coffee served at their motorhome rather than their on-track achievements. Yet, when you've had one of their knock-out espressos, you'll understand why it's more spectacular than a 12th-place finish two laps down on the race winner; but that's missing the very point of the team's existence.

However, Minardi and his co-owner Gabriele Rumi are anxious to put those days behind them, and to start to do well enough to be taken seriously at this cutting edge of motor sport – although they agree that they still plan to serve fine coffee, too...

To this end, Rumi now owns a larger share of the team than its founder, having become involved through his Fondmetal alloy-wheels business, which started supplying rims to the teams in the mid-1980s, then moved into team sponsorship and has not looked back since, even running his own team for three seasons in

the early 1990s. And it is he who is pushing for the team to be taken more seriously, with an ambitious two-year plan, to this end employing Cesare Fiono to run the outfit. Fiorio is one of the most experienced competition directors in the whole of motor sport, having guided the Lancia rally team to numerous World Championship successes before trying his hand in Formula One with Ferrari, Forti and, most recently, Prost.

The men in the cockpit

On the driving front, Minardi is sticking by Esteban Tuero, who is on a multi-year deal with the team and brings a useful budget from Argentina. He showed consistent improvement through his maiden season, which was relatively impressive for someone who won't be 21 until the end of this April, and had precious little experience before making his debut at Melbourne last March.

Likewise, Japanese driver Shinji Nakano is staying on in the team's other berth. While these drivers may not set the world alight, they are sure to improve as the season progresses, even though this appears to go against Rumi's new-found ambitions.

However, this presents Minardi with another dilemma. Does it always want to be a kindergarten team that simply schools drivers to go on to greater things with more senior teams? Ask Minardi this, and he simply smiles and says

FOR THE RECORD

Country of origin:	Italy
Team base:	Faenza, Italy
Founded:	1980
Active in Formula One:	From 1985
Grands Prix contested:	221
Grand Prix wins:	None
Pole positions:	None
Fastest laps:	None

Drivers and Results 1998

Driver	Nationality	Races	Wins	Pts	Pos
Shinji Nakano	Japanese	16	0	0	N/A
Esteban Tuero	Argentinian	16	0	0	N/A

Car specifications

Sponsors:	Fondmetal and Doimo
Team principals:	Giancarlo Minardi and Gabriele Rumi
Team manager:	Cesare Fiono
Designer:	Gustav Brunner
Chief engineer:	Gabriele Tredozi
Drivers:	Shinji Nakano and Esteban Tuero
Test driver:	tba
Chassis:	Minardi M01
Engine:	Ford VJ V10
Tyres:	Bridgestone

he gets great pleasure from their progress, as was evident when 1996 charge Fisichella snatched pole for Benetton at last year's Austrian Grand Prix. But Rumi may want to change the pattern that has seen the team score just 27 points in its 14 seasons, while unearthing a swathe of drivers that other teams didn't see fit to touch at the time. Take Alessandro Nannini, Giancarlo Fisichella and Jarno Trulli to name but a few of the drivers who graduated from his stable.

Another barren year

Tuero and team-mate Nakano failed to score a point between them for Minardi last year. Former Prost charge Nakano made the most of his extra year of Formula One experience, though, as he collected a seventh place in the Canadian Grand Prix and two eighths in the British and Belgian Grands Prix. While Tuero's highest placing was eighth in a typical race of attrition at Imola. Indeed, Nakano showed that he could simply get on with the job in hand, albeit not setting the world alight with his speed, while Tuero showed an unfortunate propensity for throwing his car off into the scenery. Still, hopefully he's learned from these over-exuberances of youth.

However, it was clear that Gabriele Tredozi's Minardi M198 chassis was a good one, as it frequently matched the pace of cars running with engines rather more powerful than the Ford V10 in the rear of the Minardis. What it could have done with a more powerful engine and a higher-ranked driver remains a matter for conjecture.

So, looking to the year ahead, matters should improve markedly, as Rumi has brought in former Ferrari designer Gustav Brunner to design the 1999 car, the Minardi M01. This will be powered not by a customer Ford engine as in 1998, but by a works one, the VJ. This will be lighter than its predecessor, have a lower crankshaft and thus a lower centre of gravity, as well as uprated electrics. So there could well be a vaulting up the order for Minardi in the season ahead, and it couldn't happen to a more deserving bunch of racers.

EASTERN PROMISE REQUIRED: Shinji Nakano will have to pull out all the stops to propel his Minardi towards the midfield, which is where the team want to be

SHINJI NAKANO

STILL TO SHINE

Shinji Nakano was the most unobtrusive driver in Formula One last season. But racing for Minardi can do that for a driver, especially if he doesn't even crash when being lapped . . .

Two seasons in Formula One, one each with Prost and Minardi, and Shinji Nakano still has to make an impression. In fact, only when he pushed Eddie Irvine's Ferrari out of the way to claim the final point at the 1997 Hungarian Grand Prix did he prick the public's consciousness. And that has to be a most unjust state of affairs. Or is it?

Taking a look at his early career, Nakano won two Japanese karting titles and spent a year in Formula Three before contesting the British Formula Vauxhall series in 1990. He raced in the Formula Vauxhall Euroseries for Paul Stewart Racing in 1991, then returned to Japan, where he moved directly to Formula 3000 with little success. He stepped down to Formula Three and rediscovered his form in 1993. Three seasons of Formula 3000 followed, with Nakano peaking with strong form in the unusual Dome chassis in 1996, claiming two second places en route to being sixth overall at the season's end.

And so to Formula One

Nakano was given a rough ride in his first season of Formula One. The problem began when the Ligier team was taken over by Alain Prost, for the four-time World Champion wanted to change a few things, such as Nakano. But Nakano had a deal that was intertwined with the supply of the team's Mugen Honda engines. And Mugen made it plain that if Prost wanted to

move Nakano aside, then it would cost the team a great deal of money.

Although not setting the world alight, he was also driving pretty well. He was unable to match team-mate Olivier Panis, but there was no disgrace in that as he was being allowed next to no testing. When much-lauded hot-shot Jarno Trulli was drafted into the team after Panis broke his legs, Nakano wasn't always left behind. Indeed, he was running three places ahead of him in the British Grand Prix before his engine blew, handing Damon Hill his first point for Arrows. Then he harried a group containing both Ferraris and Ralf Schumacher's Jordan in the Hungarian Grand Prix en route to sixth place, while Trulli finished 34 seconds behind. However, he never pulled out all the stops as Trulli did when he felt all was right.

Shinji remained in Formula One last year as a result of compatriot Ukyo Katayama quitting and leaving a ride for him at Minardi. And so he instantly lost the possibility of scoring again. But it wasn't for wont of trying, as he finished 10 of the 16 races, with a best result of seventh in the Canadian Grand Prix, backed up with a pair of eighth places and a ninth. Team-mate Esteban Tuero finished just four times, emphasizing the value of a year's experience.

ESTEBAN TUERO

LESSONS LEARNED

Esteban Tuero enjoyed a rookie Formula One season last year in which nothing was expected of him, because nobody knew who he was. This time around, he will have to step up his performance if he is to impress.

Esteban Tuero entered the record books last March at the Australian Grand Prix as the third-youngest driver ever to start a Grand Prix, at 19 years, 10 months and 16 days. Only Mike Thackwell and Ricardo Rodriguez have made the journey from cradle to cockpit any faster.

Not only was this noteworthy, but his arrival came as a massive surprise even to those who keep an eye out for up-and-coming talent, for he hadn't impressed in Formula 3000. But what he did bring was a massive budget, with which he bought a multi-year deal. And, on the evidence of his first season in Formula One, he's been learning lessons well and has never at any stage looked totally out of his depth.

Not every driver can source such a budget, but Esteban has good people behind him and a home country, Argentina, that is desperate to find a driver of its own to shine in its Grand Prix. The media exposure he's been receiving has helped Argentina's Formula One TV viewing figures, too – something that will not have escaped the attention of Formula One ringmaster Bernie Ecclestone.

Having tested for Minardi in 1997, Esteban was expected to be the team's test driver for 1998, but he joined the race line-up. Race finishes were few and far between, but eighth place at Imola was the highlight. His only yardstick was team-mate Shinji Nakano, and Esteban was not far off the more experienced Japanese driver. How he reacts to the threat of Nakano again this season remains to be seen, but expect Esteban to put his new-found experience to good use.

A few quick steps

Like most of his rivals, Esteban started in karts, doing well on the Argentinian scene. After gaining a dispensation to start racing cars at the age of 15, he competed in the national Formula Renault series in 1993, then the more powerful Formula Honda class the following year, trying his hand at Formula Three at the end of the season. He headed for Europe in 1995 and walked away with the Italian Formula 2000 series (for year-old Formula Three chassis). A season of Formula 3000 with the Draco team came next, but he never finished higher than tenth while his team-mate Ricardo Zonta won twice, emphasizing the gulf in their differing levels of talent. A season in Formula Nippon (Japan's version of Formula 3000) followed in 1997, but Esteban only once featured in the top six and quit to concentrate on test driving for Minardi and raising the budget to make his leap of faith and a Formula One campaign in 1998.

PHONE HOME: Still a teenager in 1998, Esteban calls his mother...

TRACK NOTES

Nationality: .... ARGENTINIAN
Born: .... APRIL 22, 1978,
..... BUENOS AIRES, ARGENTINA
Teams: ...... MINARDI 1998–1999

Career record

First Grand Prix: . . 1998 AUSTRALIAN
.... GRAND PRIX
Grand Prix starts: 16
Grand Prix wins: .... NONE
(best result: eighth, 1998 San Marino GP)
Poles: .... NONE
Fastest laps: .... NONE
Points: .... NONE
Honours: ... 1995 ITALIAN FORMULA 2000 CHAMPION, 1994 FORMULA HONDA ARGENTINA CHAMPION

BRITISH AMERICAN RACING

A BRAVE NEW WORLD

Tyrrell is no longer. Long live British American Racing. The 1997 World Champion, Jacques Villeneuve, thinks it's just what the sport needs, as he's signed to lead the new team.

FIGHTING TALK: Adrian Reynard predicted that BAR would win its first race in Formula One. Everyone is waiting to see

THE VIPs

Craig Pollock
Former school teacher who linked up with former pupil Jacques Villeneuve to help him advance his career when he was in Japanese Formula Three. Moved him to Toyota Atlantic series and on to first Indycars and then Formula One with remarkable success. Then dreamt up British American Racing.

Adrian Reynard
European Formula Ford 2000 Champion turned racing-car constructor. His cars have won at every level, including Indycars and Formula 3000. Accomplished water-skier and pilot. Reynard Racing Cars has received two Queen's Awards for Export Achievement.

When Stewart entered the Formula One World Championship in 1997, it was an all-new team, albeit using the experience the family had gained by running teams in the junior categories. However, this year's new team, British American Racing – BAR for short – is more of a hybrid, having taken a piggy-back on the Tyrrell team after buying it from the Tyrrell family before the start of last season. So it arrives with a year's operational experience of Formula One.

The new man at the helm, who masterminded landing British American Tobacco's multi-year involvement, is Craig Pollock, a man best known as Jacques Villeneuve's former ski teacher turned racing mentor. And he has assembled a crack squad of people around him, with Reynard implicit in the plans as being responsible for building BAR's first chassis.

Adrian Reynard has many years of Formula One experience dating back to the early 1980s, but his main successes have been in other categories from Formula Ford through to Formula 3000 to Indycars. However, he arrives with the proud boast of his cars having won the first race they've contested in each category. To do that in Formula One, though, would be a miracle, especially as the engine in the back this year will not be a works engine, but one of the less powerful Supertec (ex-Renault) engines.

Still, in Villeneuve they have a great number one driver. And it's a measure of the Canadian's confidence in his friend Pollock that he has quit Williams to join in its maiden season.

The identity of BAR's second driver took longer to sort, with Ricardo Zonta landing the deal last October. Not only does the 22-year-old

FOR THE RECORD

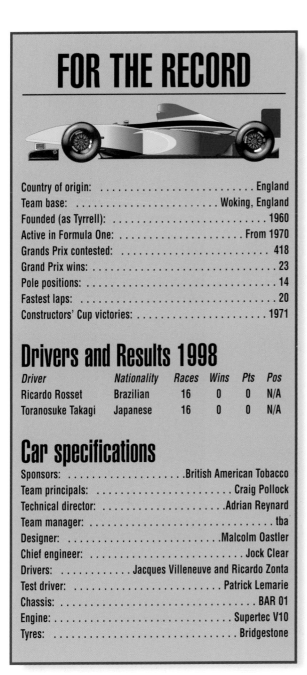

Country of origin:	England
Team base:	Woking, England
Founded (as Tyrrell):	1960
Active in Formula One:	From 1970
Grands Prix contested:	418
Grand Prix wins:	23
Pole positions:	14
Fastest laps:	20
Constructors' Cup victories:	1971

Drivers and Results 1998

Driver	Nationality	Races	Wins	Pts	Pos
Ricardo Rosset	Brazilian	16	0	0	N/A
Toranosuke Takagi	Japanese	16	0	0	N/A

Car specifications

Sponsors:	British American Tobacco
Team principals:	Craig Pollock
Technical director:	Adrian Reynard
Team manager:	tba
Designer:	Malcolm Oastler
Chief engineer:	Jock Clear
Drivers:	Jacques Villeneuve and Ricardo Zonta
Test driver:	Patrick Lemarie
Chassis:	BAR 01
Engine:	Supertec V10
Tyres:	Bridgestone

Brazilian satisfy British American Tobacco's desire to have a South American driver, but he brings useful experience from McLaren, for whom he was a test driver last season.

A sad farewell

The first definite that was laid in place for the team's last season as Tyrrell was not the choice of Ford engine, but the identity of the team's main sponsor, PIAA, which came on board in 1997 as part of a deal that saw Toranosuke Takagi become the team's test driver at the behest of former Formula One driver Satoru Nakajima. Then last year the young Japanese driver stepped up to become the team's number one after Mika Salo and Jos Verstappen moved on.

The signing of the contract for the use of Ford V10s followed. Then came the wrangling over who would drive the second car, with Verstappen, Pedro de la Rosa and Norberto Fontana all in the reckoning. But then Ricardo Rosset arrived with a bulging wallet, much to the disgust of Ken Tyrrell, who saw this as the spur to leave the team and not see through his final season before the take-over. Mind you, the thought

of Ken acting as a puppet to Pollock didn't bear thinking about.

The team also turned out with a new Ford engine. Well, the final evolution of the Ford V10 the Stewart team used in 1997, but a step or two forward from the asthmatic Ford ED4 V8 Tyrrell had used. Combined with Mike Gascoyne's aerodynamic 026 chassis, the Tyrrells were often very quick in a straight line. But, sadly, not around the fiddly bits, and thus they ended up with no points, with Takagi showing flashes of speed and a propensity to crash, while Rosset was seemingly ignored by operational head Harvey Postlethwaite, and became increasingly dejected. Neither scored a point, with Rosset's eighth place at Montreal their best showing.

The Tyrrell days

Over the past three decades, Tyrrell has been a backbone to Formula One. It was never flash or glamorous, but it helped to hold the whole thing together as a host of hopeless optimists came and went. Indeed, Ken Tyrrell ran his own team for years longer than many of today's drivers have been alive, starting off in 1968 when he fielded Jackie Stewart in a Matra. Two seasons later, with one World Drivers' Championship title in the bag, Tyrrell's own chassis came on stream and in 1971 he and Stewart claimed both the Drivers' and the Constructors' titles, with Stewart also winning the 1973 Drivers' title before retiring.

With Stewart went Tyrrell's glory days. Their passage of time together produced 25 wins (with 15 in Tyrrell chassis as opposed to the Matras and Marches that Stewart drove from 1968 to 1970), while the subsequent 25 years have offered just seven more wins – the last of these coming in Detroit in 1983. But this year is the start of a new chapter, as plain and simple Tyrrell metamorphoses into flash British American Racing.

THE VOICE OF BAR: Team founder Craig Pollock put together the sponsorship to make the team happen

JACQUES VILLENEUVE

A NEW BEGINNING

Jacques Villeneuve had a wretched year in 1998 defending his 1997 World Championship title, as Williams struggled. But he is faced with a whole new challenge for 1999, as he leads the all-new BAR team's attack.

BLOND THIS WEEK: Villeneuve sporting one of his hair colours

Jacques Villeneuve is one of the few characters in Formula One. But people should remember that he is not his father, the late Gilles Villeneuve, a driver who thrilled a generation of fans. Times have changed since he died in 1982, and the pressures a driver experiences today are far greater – which may be why Jacques remains an impish but private figure who prefers to stay out of the spotlight, even though he attracts it by constantly altering his hair colour. Jacques is truly his own man.

Jacques spent three years in Italian Formula Three. Moving to Japanese Formula Three, he was runner-up in 1992. This was followed by the North American Formula Atlantic series, with Jacques top rookie. For 1994, he raced Indycars, was sixth overall and again best rookie. He also finished second in the Indy 500, which he won in 1995, backing it up with three other wins to scoop the title.

His transition to Formula One was aided by ringmaster Bernie Ecclestone, and after a winter of testing he was set to beat Williams team-mate Damon Hill at Melbourne, and thus become the first driver since Giancarlo Baghetti in 1961 to win on his debut. But mechanical bothers made him settle for second. However, he won four races and pushed Hill for the title.

Becoming World Champion

It looked as though Jacques wouldn't win the 1997 world title, as after seven races he had just three wins, but the other four races had ended in retirement, and Ferrari's Michael Schumacher was on a winning streak. Jacques then inherited wins in the British and Hungarian Grands Prix. Yet fifth places at Spa and Monza showed all was not well. But he won twice after Mika Hakkinen and Jarno Trulli slowed in Austria, and then Hakkinen and David Coulthard blew up ahead of him at the Nurburgring. Better still, Schumacher was taken off at the first corner, allowing Jacques to go to Suzuka needing only to score a point for the title. But he was disqualified after taking pole position, and had to race under appeal, taking the title race to the final race at Jerez. But there he survived an aggressive clash with Schumacher, and third was enough to give him the world title.

Last year was a struggle, as the McLarens and then the Ferraris left the Williams cars in their wake. But Jacques earned respect for the way in which he never gave less than 100 per cent in a car that was a real handful. By mid-season it looked less liable to leap into the scenery, and Jacques was on the podium for third place at both the German and Hungarian Grands Prix. But by then his deal to move on to British American Racing was signed.

TRACK NOTES

Nationality: . . . . .CANADIAN
Born: . . . . APRIL 9, 1971,
.ST JEAN-SUR-RICHELIEU, CANADA
Teams: . . . . . WILLIAMS 1996–1998,
. . . . BAR 1999

Career record

First Grand Prix: 1996 AUSTRALIAN GP
Grand Prix starts: 49
Grand Prix wins: 11
(1996 European GP, 1996 British GP, 1996 Hungarian GP, 1996 Portuguese GP, 1997 Brazilian GP, 1997 Argentinian GP, 1997 Spanish GP, 1997 British GP, 1997 Hungarian GP, 1997 Austrian GP, 1997 Luxembourg GP)
Poles: 13
Fastest laps: 9
Points: 180
Honours: . . 1997 WORLD CHAMPION, 1996 FORMULA ONE RUNNER-UP, 1995 INDYCAR CHAMPION, 1994 INDYCAR ROOKIE OF THE YEAR, 1993 TOYOTA ATLANTIC ROOKIE OF THE YEAR, 1992 JAPANESE FORMULA THREE RUNNER-UP

RICARDO ZONTA

THE NEW STAR

Ricardo Zonta is a shy and unassuming individual. But put him behind the wheel of a racing car and he's dynamite, as his championship-laden track record shows. Expect him to fly for the new BAR team.

TRACK NOTES

Nationality: . . . . BRAZILIAN
Born: . . . . MARCH 23, 1976,
. . . . CURITIBA, BRAZIL
Teams: . . . . BAR 1999

Career record
First Grand Prix: 1999 AUSTRALIAN GP
Grand Prix starts: . . . . NONE
Grand Prix wins: . . . . N/A
    Poles: . . . . NONE
Fastest laps: . . . . NONE
Points: . . . . NONE
Honours: . . 1998 FIA GT CHAMPION,
1997 FORMULA 3000 CHAMPION, 1995
SOUTH AMERICAN AND BRAZILIAN
FORMULA 3 CHAMPION

When Ricardo Zonta came to Europe as the reigning South American Formula Three Champion in 1996, he was something of a mystery, having risen so fast through the racing ranks in his native Brazil that people didn't really know who he was. Unable to speak anything other than Portuguese, he wasn't able to tell people either, so he let his driving do the talking – with good effect – and was the Formula 3000 rookie of the year, finishing fourth overall after a late-season charge netted two wins.

Small wonder, then, that he was selected to race for the crack Super Nova team in his second season in the category, and duly became champion by winning three times to edge out Juan Pablo Montoya. Actually, he won four times, but his first win was taken away from him on a technicality. This performance impressed enough to land him the McLaren test ride, along with Nick Heidfeld.

Fast and furious
Loyal to their charges, McLaren's engine supplier Mercedes placed him with its works GT team, and Ricardo took to this with typical aplomb, partnering sportscar veteran Klaus Ludwig to wins in the first round at Oscherlseben, Dijon-Prenois, the A1-Ring, Homestead and Laguna Seca en route to winning the FIA GT Championship. He ruffled a few feathers, but this was as much to do with his natural speed as his occasionally over-exuberant driving.

However, Ricardo was also gaining useful testing experience with McLaren, impressing greatly when he topped the timesheets in a massed test session at Magny-Cours in France last September, even outpacing the experienced McLaren drivers David Coulthard and Mika Hakkinen.

Landing the deal
For all this form as a test driver, though, McLaren decided to keep the same driver line-up for 1999, and so he was forced to look elsewhere for a ride for the season ahead. Rumours linked him with a ride with Minardi so that he could cut his teeth driving for a junior team before moving up to McLaren's Formula One line-up.

But then came the start of a deal with the new BAR team, with sponsors and co-owners British American Tobacco favouring a South American driver in the second car alongside lead driver Jacques Villeneuve.

All looked set, but then Ricardo's ride suddenly looked under threat when his wealthy compatriot Pedro Diniz tired of the Arrows team and started to look elsewhere, but Ricardo held on and landed the drive.

Certainly, he will have to shine to outrace Villeneuve, but Ricardo is a smooth and very fast driver who could prove one of the bright lights of the year ahead, providing the first BAR car is up to scratch.

A WINNING SMILE: Ricardo Zonta is a winner in everything he races

OTHER DRIVERS

WAITING IN THE WINGS

Ignore the ranks of Formula One test drivers at your peril, as Mika Hakkinen, Damon Hill and David Coulthard have all served their time in this role before going on to bigger and better things.

ONE FOR THE FUTURE: Juan Pablo Montoya could be a future champion

The Formula One World Championship is as frantic off the track as it is on it, with wheeling-and-dealing galore – especially when it comes to sorting out who drives for whom in the following season. And, inevitably, when the music stops, a few worthy souls are left clutching their helmets and little else. Some will make do with a test role with one of the leading teams, while others will be left with nothing.

Reigning World Champion Mika Hakkinen was so desperate to quit the ailing Lotus team for McLaren for the 1993 season that he signed up without being sure that a drive was even available. When Ayrton Senna decided to settle his differences and sign for McLaren, Hakkinen was left as the team's test driver. However, this proved to be the best move of his career, as it got his foot in the door of one of the sport's top teams. And you don't win Grands Prix without driving for one of the top few teams.

Hakkinen's team-mate David Coulthard made his way into Formula One with the Williams test team before getting his break with the race team after Senna's death in 1994, joining forces with Damon Hill who had already graduated to the race team from the test team at the start of the previous season. Emphasizing the benefits of being with a top team, Hill was able to take a serious tilt at winning the title in his second season, whereas had he not taken the test team route and expended his efforts on landing a race ride at all costs, he would probably have ended up at the back of the grid. So for the lucky few, it works, and cuts out years of endeavour and heartbreak.

Looking at the testing berths with the top teams, Ricardo Zonta has moved up from McLaren's test team to race for BAR this

season, but McLaren and Mercedes were so impressed with him that they want an option on his services for the future. His fellow 1998 McLaren test driver, Nick Heidfeld, was pipped to last year's Formula 3000 title, and will make another bid for it with McLaren's junior team, West Competition. However, Heidfeld will continue to log the laps in the team's Formula One cars, helping both the team and himself.

Ferrari tends to view its test driver as someone who is not so much a part of its future plans, as one who can carry out useful testing work and step into the race team should either Michael Schumacher or Eddie Irvine be injured. To this end, Ferrari has former Formula One driver Luca Badoer as a capable backstop.

Williams used both Juan Pablo Montoya – the driver who beat Heidfeld to the Formula 3000 title – and fellow Formula 3000 racer Max Wilson last year. But, with Montoya having gone to race Champ Cars, and with double Champ Car champion Alessandro Zanardi and Ralf Schumacher new to the team, it is unlikely that Williams will run a test team, instead giving the job to the incomers so that they can enjoy as much mileage as possible. Montoya, thwarted in his ambitions of moving up to Williams' race team, is down to spend a season or two in Champ Cars. But this doesn't mean that he won't eventually work his way back to Formula One. After all, a three-year spell Stateside has turned Zanardi into a hot property welcomed back to Formula One with open arms. Which is markedly different to the way in which he was perceived when he left with little fanfare at the end of 1994.

Jordan has used the talented Spaniard Pedro de la Rosa for its testing duties, but his hopes of moving up to the race team were thwarted when Heinz-Harald Frentzen filled the second seat.

Stewart Grand Prix makes the most of its junior team, and will be using Mario Haberfeld – who won the team its umpteenth British Formula Three title last year – as its test driver. However, the team is keen to let everyone know that this is not so much to do with its loyalty to him but with his ability at the wheel. So, watch this space.

The majority of the teams in the second half of the grid don't do enough testing to make it worth paying a test driver. But they are only too happy if someone desperate for mileage in a Formula One car pays for the privilege, leaving the way open for a few ambitious young guns, such as Laurent Redon with Minardi.

There will be extra testing berths in the year ahead as Honda gears up to re-enter Formula One in the year 2000, with Jos Verstappen landing this plum ride. Likewise, Jorg Muller has moved across from Sauber to be BMW's test driver.

FLYING SCOT: Dario Franchitti is biding his time in Champ Car racing

Formula 3000 heroes

Not all drivers trying to land a ride in Formula One come from the ranks of test drivers, though, as there simply aren't enough places. So keep a look-out, too, for those racing in Formula 3000 (Formula One's feeder formula with all its races now on the Grand Prix support programme) – especially those with the McLaren and Prost junior teams – as well as the pick of the crop in Champ Car racing; there are quite a few people there who could do as good a job as some of the drivers in Formula One.

In fact, there is one driver waiting in the wings who has yet to make his Formula One debut, but who has led more Grand Prix laps than many Formula One veterans lead in their entire career: Oliver Gavin. A sometime test driver with Benetton and a Formula 3000 star, he has spent the past two years driving the safety car at Grands Prix, being called out to lead the field around when conditions have

STILL WAITING: Pedro de la Rosa was Jordan's 1998 test driver

THE LEADER: Oliver Gavin deserves to step up from the safety car

become too tricky for racing or while accident debris is cleaned off the circuit. It will be tragic waste if he's never given the chance to try and lead a Grand Prix in a Formula One car.

If you want to watch for the stars of tomorrow, keep an eye out for the progress of French drivers Soheil Ayari and Stephane Sarrazin, as well as Uruguay's Gonzalo Rodriguez and smiling Dane Jason Watt. Flying Scot Dario Franchitti is also on the look-out for a move from Champ Cars, perhaps for the year after this. His Champ Car contemporary Greg Moore may also head for Formula One, to prove there is more than one top driver from Canada.

Openings don't happen very often in Formula One, especially when you consider the likes of Jean Alesi lining up for his tenth full season of Formula One. But there's nothing so rewarding as watching the progress of the best drivers in Formula 3000 and the categories below, observing how they make it to the top, and thus knowing precisely who they are when they spring out into the limelight.

Taking the strain...

TECHNICAL INSIGHT

60

Formula 1 cars present one of the most hostile working environments imaginable for thousands of intricate and sophisticated components and must be able to withstand a rapid-fire onslaught of twists, bumps and buffeting.

By its very nature, motor racing demands that the car you produce must be fast, but without durability, any 'success' in speed acheivement will be short-lived.

To the average road-going car, a lap around any race track would feel like driving across a billiard table. In an F1 car, however, that same lap might feel just as smooth and comfortable as taking the family hatchback for a spin through a building site! Benetton's Chief Designer, Nick Wirth, reveals some of the major implications of car stress and how these problems are tackled...

Graphic: © Russell Lewis

Every which way...

The main sources of stress stem from exerted g-forces. Capable of flying from zero to 160km/h and back to a standstill in little more than six seconds, it is not difficult to appreciate the forces that shudder through the car.

These pressures are more than matched by the lateral strains of high-speed cornering. Forces of around 3g, in all directions, will be experienced at the Nürburgring – this can reach 4.0g on the high-speed circuits

Flicking through fast, sweeping sections like Silverstone's Maggotts complex or Suzuka's S Curves, for example, piles on the pressure in every direction...

4: Gravity does its best to 'throw' everything off the back of the car under acceleration!

1: Stress loadings under braking are around 3-4 times greater than under maximum acceleration.
This is a problem that has increased significantly since the introduction of highly-efficient carbon brakes

2/3: As loadings shift from a straightline approach, cars must be capable of 'hanging' on lateral forces in excess of 3.5g.
Stress peaks as loadings switch rapidly from side to side

The fifth dimension — taking a dip...

The beam stiffness – resistance to 'bending' in the middle – is very high in comparison to suspension stiffness. This rigidity allows the car to move only through its suspension range, settling on springs, dampers and tyres as the downward force is absorbed

A bit of bump n grind...

As slow-motion TV pictures confirm, cars take a pounding as drivers attempt to shave fractions of seconds from lap times by 'riding' the kerbs. Stress loads through the suspension can be equivalent to four times the car's static weight on 'landing'!

P Positive kerb

Direction of travel

N Negative kerb

x4

Positive (P): Used on curve apices.
Negative (N): 'mirror' of positive profile, used on exits to prevent cars 'lifting'. This is the most 'aggressive' kerb type and has the greatest effect in terms of car stress due to the high levels of vibration it can generate

A life in a day of F1

Sixteen or seventeen times a year, the F1 grid rolls out to do battle, the same familiar helmets in the cockpits, the same cars – or are they? While many of the cars' component parts are designed to last the whole season, others may only survive a few races – or less! Benetton Operations and Team Manager, Joan Villadeprat, reveals the secrets of the incredible turnover in the F1 'spares department' and why, beneath the surface, the cars you see in later races have so little of their original hardware on board...

For the record: for telemetry sensors in areas prone to excessive vibration or heat – e.g. wheel hubs/exhaust – life can be as little as 500km. Others can last 3,000km

KEY **0** Component life (number of races*) **S** Full season component life

Driving forces...

Engine: returned to Mecachrome for servicing after each Grand Prix
Gearbox: gearbox casting will normally survive the whole season, new ratios and bearings will last for just a single race, while differentials and main motion shafts can go through two or three Grands Prix
Clutch: designed to withstand one race start – hence the nervousness when re-starts are called! Stripped and serviced after each race
Lubricants: changed after each session

Steering wheel: while mechanical parts, such as gear-shift paddles will last for around half of the season, electronic components within the unit may last variously from two to five GPs

Checkin' wings...

UNITED COLORS OF BENETTON.

All wings and other aerodynamic components are routinely checked for cracks or heat-damage and replaced as necessary. New undertrays are manufactured for each race

MILD SEVEN

Radiators: replaced every second race

Cars stripped and re-sprayed and stickers replaced after each race

Braking point...

Calipers will see out a full season, discs and pads are good for just one race

Full circle...

In 'routine' running, wheels have a lifespan of around 4,000km – equivalent to five Grands Prix

Exhaust: one of few parts replaced as a matter of course after every race, regardless of condition

Refuelling: all components, including fuel pump, serviced after each race. Rings, filters and seals are replaced on car and hoses
On-board computers: main ECU is switched after each race

Suspended sentence...

Within the complex suspension system – up to 50 configurations are possible – coils will last the full year, while dampers are serviced after each race. Wishbones will normally be used for three Grands Prix

In the hot seat...

Each driver will use five or six custom-built carbon-fibre seats throughout the year, checked regularly for cracks or fatigue...

...and each will have twelve sets of fireproof overalls (six with tobacco branding and six 'non-tobacco') and six new crash helmets. Seat belts will last the season

'Grand Prix' refers to Friday, Saturday and Sunday running (650kms approx) / 'Race' means race only (300kms approx)

Benetton's wheel of fortune

Since the 'paddle' gear-shift mechanism first appeared on the steering wheel of a sceptical Nigel Mansell's Ferrari in Brazil, 1989, an inestimable amount of time and money has been invested in turning one of the car's most basic components into a major nerve-centre.

Today's drivers have both hands firmly fixed to a technological masterpiece that is worth rather more than its weight in gold!

Function mode (±): works in conjuction with main function selector switch, button scrolls *down* through setting options. '(+)' button scrolls *up*

So what are all those flashing lights and buttons about? Read on as all is revealed...

Traffic signals: lights set in top of steering wheel give a constant guide to car's running status

`SL' (Gear shift): sequential lights pre-set to specific 'rev' bands – determined by individual circuit characteristics and conditions – tell drivers when to change gear

A/D:	Spare
B/C:	Pit lane speed limiter on
E:	Radio indicator
F/H:	Clutch (separate left and right paddle indicators)
G:	Throttle. Pre-sets allow indication of optimum throttle level for start
J:	Second pit limiter indicator

Reverse gear: on the back of the steering wheel...

1: Gear up-shift
2: Gear down-shift
3/4: Clutch paddles

The right connections: wheel 'plugs in' to the car via a set of pins that lock into corresponding sockets on the tip of the steering column

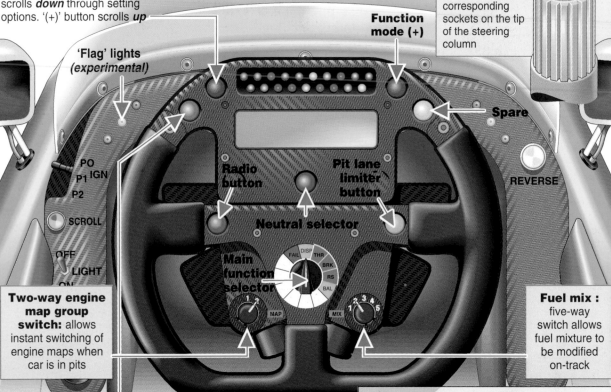

Function mode (+)

'Flag' lights *(experimental)*

Spare

PO
P1 IGN
P2

SCROLL

OFF
LIGHT
ON

Radio button

Pit lane limiter button

Neutral selector

REVERSE

Main function selector

Two-way engine map group switch: allows instant switching of engine maps when car is in pits

Fuel mix : five-way switch allows fuel mixture to be modified on-track

Logger switch: Should a problem occur on-track, button can 'mark' telemetry read-out for later analysis by engineers

Main function switch: determines which data is displayed on screen and activates selected programme

DISP: scrolls display of pressure data on various circuits such as compressed air and brakes

FAIL: simulates selected component failure – used for testing only!

BAL: sets front-to-rear brake balance (15 settings)

Engine data and settings

THR: controls throttle function to Mecachrome specifications (5 settings)

BRK: controls engine braking effect to preserve rear brakes (5 settings)

RS: spare channel for Mechachrome settings

Screen display: a massive range of data can be displayed on integral screen. Illustration below represents a 'typical' on-track display

Error ID: if a fault develops on-track, driver can radio number to engineers. Using this code, the team can indentify the problem and tell the driver if it is safe to continue or if he must pit

Engine revs — Speed (km/h)

Gear   Lap time – *display will flash to indicate a best time*   Water temp.

The F1 time trial...

While media and spectator attention in F1 tends to remain firmly focused on the race track, the activity 'behind the scenes' to ensure that cars are ready for the grid is no less frenetic.

Given that many of the cars' components have a very short lifespan, there is a lot of 'routine' work to be done. Timing in the workshops and trackside garages – as on the track itself – is critical and it is tight! Consider the man-hours taken, under normal circumstances, to get a car ready to race and you begin to understand the despair of the 'unsung heroes' when cars get bent!

In the F1 workplace there are two versions of 'time'. Away from the track, work is carried out under controlled conditions. During race weekends, this gives way to urgency – at times, even desperation. A job that can take a day at 'home' may have to be done in an hour trackside...

Aerodynamic components: service, check for cracks, repair/replace

On-board computers: service, swap between units

Electronics looms: maintenance to, or switching (two sets per car available)

Refuelling components: replace rings, filters and seals after each race, service fuel pump. *(Rigs serviced by manufacturer)*

Steering wheel: Regular checking and maintenance of electronic and mechanical components. Two days to assemble from 'scratch'

Brakes: new discs and pads fitted for each race. Between three and four hours to assemble and fit

Suspension: service dampers, replace worn or damaged wishbones (full car set)

Gear ratios: new for each race, removing gearbox and inserting a set of ratios takes around two hours. Gearbox is refitted to car in around 10 minutes.

Post-race: strip, service, ultra-sonic cleaning and unit re-build

Engine: complete post-race strip and re-build – by the engine manufacturer – takes around 150 hours.

Engine changes on the car vary according to the level of preparation. A 'ready' engine, with its major external components fixed, can be fitted in around two and a half hours.

A 'prepared' engine – with all hoses, fittings, leads etc. in place – can be fitted in 45-60 minutes!

Sponsor logos: sticker placement has to be exact – everything in its correct position and squared up! Replacing a full set can take anything up to five hours

The F1 strip-show...

A typical F1 car consists of more than 12,000 component parts. Such is the precision of F1 team-work that a complete car can be stripped, serviced and re-built within five days. When pushed – providing that all parts are ready – it is not unheard of for a team to turn a car around in just a day-and-a-half!

Time to go home...

When the racing ends the packing begins. At 'flyaway' races the teams will have as much as 18 tonnes of equipment with them! – and every last item of this will be packed away in its own place.

Every racing fan has a favourite driver. But, equally, every fan also has a favourite circuit. It may be their local Grand Prix venue, or it may simply be one that has produced great races over the years. But there are a handful of circuits that merit mention time after time, especially in this day and age when many of the great tracks of old have been emasculated in the name of safety.

Indeed, while circuits like Silverstone, Spa-Francorchamps and Suzuka are at the top of many people's lists, others have slid down the rankings since the introduction of safety measures such as chicanes, which have broken up their natural flow. On the other hand, new circuits tend to stick to a formula that includes too many slow corners,

making it hard for drivers to overtake. Steps were made to correct this for 1998, with the cars running in narrower trim and on grooved tyres in a quest to make it easier to pass, other than during pit stops. Sadly, while the cars were more spectacular to watch, sliding around on the limit, it was hard to spot any extra overtaking.

By general consensus, Silverstone, Spa-Francorchamps and Suzuka are not just the most exciting circuits to drive around, but have also hosted some of the best Grands Prix ever. They have seen Mansell go head-to-head with Piquet, Schumacher against Villeneuve and Prost versus Senna. To most, Spa-Francorchamps is the pick of the bunch. It sweeps through Belgium's forested Ardennes hills, offering a mix of high-speed corners and a lap long enough

to get stuck into. And no corner earns more respect than Eau Rouge. Approached downhill, with a left-right flick on the entry, it immediately shoots steeply up again with the drivers trying to keep their throttles planted. It never fails to impress.

Silverstone used to be the fastest circuit of all, but its nature has changed many times since it hosted the first modern-day Grand Prix in 1950, with slower corners having been inserted in recent years. However, the Becketts sweepers are a must and Bridge corner always excites. Furthermore, Silverstone is steeped in history and is also fun to attend, as it's the home Grand Prix for most of the teams, and they let rip in a massive post-race party.

Japan's Suzuka circuit is one on which a driver with talent can make a difference.

MELBOURNE BUENOS AIRES INTERLAGOS IMOLA MON
A-1 RING   HOCKENHEIM   HUNGARORING   SPA-FRANC

F1 KNOW THE TRACKS

With its visit coming at the end of the season, though, its delights are often obscured by the all-consuming world title showdown.

And what of the others? Monaco is one that every race fan wants to visit. Like Spa-Francorchamps, Monaco is steeper than television makes it look, and far narrower. It would be hard enough driving it alone, but to race alongside others means a driver can never relax. And if it rains, as it did last in 1996, those barriers are lying in wait.

If you are looking for a circuit rich in tradition, then a pilgrimage to Monza for the Italian Grand Prix is a must. Not only does it offer some wonderful high-speed spectating points, but you can take a look at the banked corners that were used until the 1950s. You only realize how steep they are when you try to walk up them, and it certainly gives you a renewed respect for the heroes of the day, who used to hit speeds of close on 200mph on this original circuit in their Alfa Romeos, Mercedes and Maseratis.

While on the subject of defunct parts of current Grand Prix circuits, the public roads that used to be part of Spa-Francorchamps are still clear to anyone with a road map. And the Nurburgring Nordschleife remains a closed circuit that is open to the public – for the price of a light meal, you can take your own car out for a blast around its awesome 14-mile lap.

The Albert Park circuit is popular, as it's right next to the attractions of downtown Melbourne, much as the Circuit Gilles Villeneuve is located close to the heart of the cosmopolitan city of Montreal.

The calendar could have two additions this year, with Formula One making its first visit to Malaysia and possibly to China which is listed as a reserve. The all-new Sepang circuit in Malaysia is a facility that appears not to offer any great challenge, with its mix of slow corners. What it does offer, though, is great viewing from its massive grandstands. Unfortunately, it should also provide the drivers and teams with the hottest working environment of the season. China's Zhuhai circuit is three years old and has hosted races in the FIA's GT series.

So, despite Formula One's prevailing homogenization, there is still great variety in the circuits used in the current World Championship calendar, with every Grand Prix having a character of its own.

BARCELONA MONTREAL MAGNY-COURS SILVERSTONE
HAMPS MONZA NURBURGRING SEPANG SUZUKA

MELBOURNE

Australian Grand Prix
M E L B O U R N E

Circuit length: **5.302km**
Race distance: **58 laps**

Albert Park

March
7

Hill
Ascari
Stewart
Waite
Prost
Clark Chicane
Lauda
Marina
Albert
Road
Brabham
Jones
Whiteford
Timing sectors

ROUND 1   MARCH 7, 1999

Melbourne's Albert Park has hosted just three Grands Prix, but already this fast and flowing circuit around a lake has the feel of being one of Formula One's classic venues.

Albert Park, Melbourne: 3.274 miles/5.302km; 58 laps. Lap record: Heinz-Harald Frentzen (Williams-Renault), 1m 30.585s, 130.929mph,1997

1998 Results	
1 Mika Hakkinen	McLaren
2 David Coulthard	McLaren
3 Heinz-Harald Frentzen	Williams
4 Eddie Irvine	Ferrari
5 Jacques Villeneuve	Williams
6 Johnny Herbert	Sauber

Three-time World Champion Jack Brabham had to turn his back on his native Australia in the 1950s, and head to Europe to get on to the ladder that took him to Formula One. But times have changed and Australia has been an integral part of the World Championship since 1985, when Adelaide opened its arms to Formula One. Add to this the fact that the race has seldom failed to provide high

READY FOR THE OFF: The McLarens line up first and second. And this was as close as the opposition came

excitement since then, and you can understand why so many fans make the journey.

Adelaide was small and cosy, and everyone in Formula One loved going there during the South Australian city's 11-year spell of hosting the race up until 1995. The party atmosphere was helped no end by it being the last race of the year, and thus it was the perfect time to go wild.

Mansell's monster moment

Adelaide also meant spectacular racing. Who can forget the season-closer in 1986 when it all went wrong for Nigel Mansell? 'Our Nige', his Williams team-mate Nelson Piquet and McLaren's Alain Prost were going for the title when Mansell had his monster blow-out and snaked off up an escape road just as he moved into a position of control, leaving Prost to win the race and the title.

There was more drama in 1989 when the race was stopped almost before it had started because of torrential rain, but not before many cars had aquaplaned into the surrounding concrete walls or into each other. Amazingly for a country that is predominantly arid, rain hit again in 1991.

For many, the race at Adelaide that will always stick in the mind is the 1994 showdown between Michael Schumacher and Damon Hill. Coming under pressure for the lead from Hill, Schumacher's Benetton clipped one of the surrounding walls. Then, just as Hill tried to dive by, the German closed the door and was pitched off. Sadly for Hill, he too was out, his Williams limping to the pits with damaged suspension, and so the title went to Schumacher.

And so to Melbourne

Adelaide may have been fun, but the state of Victoria is the home of the Australian motorsport industry, so it was only right that its capital, Melbourne, should take over the Grand Prix. And so it did in 1996, albeit as the season-opener. It almost provided one of the biggest shocks ever in Formula One, as Jacques Villeneuve was set to win on his debut (only achieved previously by Giancarlo Baghetti, for Ferrari in 1961), but his oil pressure dropped and he was advised to slow down, letting Williams team-mate Hill through to win.

Melbourne's Albert Park circuit is unlike Adelaide's street circuit in that it's all in a park, making its layout more flowing. Running clockwise around a lake, the circuit begins with an 'ess' that's approached at 180mph, leading into the second-gear right-hander where Martin Brundle

destroyed his car in 1996. Then the track keeps bending right and the drivers hit fifth gear before a second-gear chicane, then sixth and up to over 170mph before another 'ess'. Into the back section, now sweeping left, drivers see 180mph before they take a pair of right-handers around the far end of the lake, before completing the lap with a second-gear left-hander and a quicker right on to the main straight.

The second visit to Melbourne looked as though Villeneuve would walk it for Williams after he had dominated qualifying. But he was taken out by Eddie Irvine at the first corner, and so David Coulthard was able to race on to McLaren's first win since Adelaide in 1993, with Heinz-Harald Frentzen crashing out of second place in the closing laps. It was also a race that gave Hill a clue his season was not going to go smoothly, as his Arrows coasted to a halt on the parade lap, meaning he didn't even take the start for the first race of his World Championship title defence.

Melbourne in 1998 marked the start of McLaren's initially dominant year, with Hakkinen and Coulthard leaving the opposition in their wake. But even winning by such a large margin left a bad taste in the mouths of some, as Hakkinen thought mistakenly that he had been called into the pits and thus lost the lead. Coulthard, though, stuck to a pre-race agreement that whichever of them entered the first corner in the lead at the start would win the race, and so he slowed and let Hakkinen through with three laps to go. Race promoter Ron Walker hit the roof, but then he finds a reason to do so every year. For the record, Frentzen was a lap down in third.

HERO OF THE TRACK

Melbourne's Alan Jones has racing blood in his veins. And he's still racing V8 saloons at the age of 52. Son of racer Stan Jones, Alan lived hand-to-mouth to finance his Formula Three races in Europe in the 1970s, but it paid off and he advanced to Formula One in 1975 with a private Hesketh. Drives with Hill, Surtees and Shadow followed, and his maiden win for Shadow in Austria in 1977 helped him move to Williams. Then the wins started to flow, and he quit Formula One with 12 victories to his name and the 1980 World Championship.

BUENOS AIRES

ROUND 2   MARCH 28, 1999

Some circuits are fast and flowing; others, like the Buenos Aires circuit, are tight and twisty — which is a shame, as the original circuit was a mighty one with plenty of high-speed sweepers.

Argentina's Juan Manuel Fangio is the most successful driver ever to have raced in Formula One, collecting five World Championship titles in the 1950s. Yet, for all the impetus he and subsequent heroes such as Carlos Reutemann provided, Argentina remains a bit player in world motorsport, its beleaguered economy leaving it lagging behind nations with a lesser claim to motorsport supremacy throughout the 1970s and 1980s. This is why it's having to play catch-up, and its premier circuit has had to be rebuilt to bring it up to contemporary Formula One requirements. As this happened immediately after Ayrton Senna died at Imola in 1994, that meant a rush to insert slow corners rather than the wonderfully open, fast ones that used to be such a characteristic of the track. For all this chopping about, though, at least the circuit of the city of Buenos Aires remains one of the world's most beguiling.

Back on the map

Argentina has only recently returned to the Formula One calendar after years in the wilderness. Home of Fangio and Jose Froilan Gonzalez, the country was a hub of motor racing in the 1950s, with Grands Prix as well as non-championship races being held during the Northern Hempishere's winter. Demonstrating racing's staggering popularity in South America, Fangio drew in hundreds of thousands of fans for what they hoped would be a triumphant homecoming for the country's first Grand Prix in 1953. On that occasion it didn't work out, as Italian Alberto Ascari won for Ferrari, but Fangio won the race on the next four occasions and the race remained on the calendar until 1960, with the exception of 1959. However, by then Argentina's trickle of talent to Europe dried up and the race was not held again until 1972, when local ace Reutemann took pole position in his Brabham, but couldn't stop Jackie Stewart from winning in his Tyrrell.

With the exception of 1976, when political unrest led to its cancellation, the race ran until 1981 – usually as the season-opener as part of a two-race package with the Brazilian Grand Prix. To the disappointment of the crowd, Reutemann was destined never to win his home Grand Prix, with second place in both 1979 and 1981 his best results there.

It was only in 1995 that the Formula One circus visited Argentina again, sadly to the much-emasculated track used today. Still, Damon Hill clearly loves it, as he won there two years on the trot for Williams. The Williams team took the spoils again in 1997, with Jacques Villeneuve able to suppress a bout of Montezuma's Revenge sufficiently to resist a late challenge from Eddie Irvine's Ferrari to win by a car's length. After a cracking start to the season, a third consecutive McLaren one-two was expected last year, perhaps with pole-sitter David Coulthard taking the spoils. But they hadn't expected Michael Schumacher to be in such attacking form for Ferrari, and he tipped Coulthard out of the lead before going on to win.

Right, left, right

A lap of the circuit is now a stop-start procedure, with drivers having to be extremely careful at the first corner, Curva Numero Uno, for this is a tightening right-hander approached at 180mph. Even though the track and the grass verges are wide, there can be trouble there, as was witnessed in 1995 when Jean Alesi locked up, spinning into the middle of the pack with costly consequences.

Unusually, Michael Schumacher made a mistake there in 1997, triggering a chain-reaction that saw cars spinning everywhere.

Out of the first corner, the drivers run through a fourth-gear kink into a left-hand hairpin. Up through the gearbox from second, there's a left

TIGHT AND SLOW: Mika Salo guides his Arrows through the circuit's narrow twists in last year's Grand Prix

Argentine Grand Prix
B U E N O S   A I R E S

BRAZIL

Buenos
Aires

**March
28**

Circuit length: 4.259km
Race distance: 72 laps

Curva
Numero Uno

Curvón

Curva del
Ombú

Curva de la
Confiteria

Viborita

Senna 'S'

Curva de
Ascari

Horquilla

Entrada a
los Mixtos

Timing sectors

Argentinian Grand Prix
Buenos Aires: 2.646
miles/4.259km, 72 laps.
Lap record: Gerhard Berger
(Benetton-Renault), 1m 27.981s,
108.290mph, 1997

1998 results
1 Michael Schumacher   Ferrari
2 Mika Hakkinen   Benetton
3 Eddie Irvine   Ferrari
4 Alexander Wurz   Benetton
5 Jean Alesi   Sauber
6 David Coulthard   McLaren

HERO OF THE TRACK

Few people today can imagine the impact that Juan Manuel Fangio had on Formula One in the 1950s. Not only did he win the world title five times – in 1951, 1954, 1955, 1956 and 1957 – but he presented an air of invincibility. And he did this at an age that seems barely credible today, for he was 46 when he won his last title. What's more, this was when the cars were far heavier to drive than they are today, and the races longer. Fangio, who died in 1995, was a real hero.

corner, the 160mph Ascarı bend. Sadly, another second-gear hairpin follows to break the flow, then a double-apex left, the Senna esses and finally the tight Horquilla right-hander on to the pit straight. No wonder some drivers refer to it as a kart track...

With Reutemann now a state senator and promising greater things yet in the Argentinian government, the future of the race looks secure, and there are a host of up-and-coming Argentinian drivers headed by Esteban Tuero lining up for a crack at Formula One, hoping to become a latter-day Reutemann.

then a long right on to the back straight. Getting the exit of this corner right is crucial as the following straight leads into the track's fastest

A CITY BACKDROP: The Buenos Aires skyline is in the background when you look down the back straight

INTERLAGOS

ROUND 3   APRIL 11, 1999

Few circuits have more passionate fans than Interlagos. But their fanaticism has been dimmed of late as they haven't found heroes of their own to cheer since the passing of Ayrton Senna.

Brazilian Grand Prix
I N T E R L A G O S

Circuit length: 4.292km
Race distance: 72 laps

São Paulo

April 11

Arquibancadas

Subida

Cotovêlo

Laranja

Junção

Pinheirinho   Mergulho

Ferradura

Descida
do Lago

Reta Oposta

Curva 1

Senna's S

Curva
do Sol

Timing sectors

Interlagos, Sao Paulo:
2.660 miles/4.292km;
72 laps. Lap record:
Jacques Villeneuve (Williams-
Renault), 1m 18.397s,
122.471mph, 1997

1998 results
1 Mika Hakkinen	McLaren
2 David Coulthard	McLaren
3 Michael Schumacher	Ferrari
4 Alexander Wurz	Benetton
5 Heinz-Harald Frentzen	Williams
6 Giancarlo Fisichella	Benetton

BEST OF THE REST: Ferrari's Michael Schumacher had to make do with a distant third place behind the McLarens

Amazingly for a country that can number multiple Formula One World Champions Emerson Fittipaldi, Nelson Piquet and Ayrton Senna among its ranks, Brazil remains on the periphery, thousands of miles away from the sport's axis in Europe. Indeed, anyone who makes the journey to Sao Paulo to watch the Grand Prix at Interlagos will understand the difference. And it's not just Sao Paulo's soaring temperatures that stand out; it's the people, as the whole country is totally Formula One mad – even the ultra-poor who live in the shanty towns that spring up on every vacant plot. The lucky ones who can afford entry to the circuit bring with them a carnival spirit that not even Europe's liveliest crowd at Imola can match.

Brazil found a place on the Formula One map after the first of its hotshot drivers, Emerson Fittipaldi, burst on to the racing scene in Europe in 1969. After hosting a non-championship race won by Carlos Reutemann in 1972, Interlagos became home to the Brazilian Grand Prix from 1973, its grandstands packed with flag-waving enthusiasts who, on scorching days, would be doused with water to prevent them from overheating.

Interlagos was initially a lengthy track, with a fast, open section around the perimeter linking to a twisting infield around a lake. The drivers loved its challenge and the early years were kind to the local crowds, as local hero Fittipaldi won in 1973 and 1974, for Lotus and McLaren respectively. In 1975, another Brazilian won, this time Carlos Pace proving victorious for Brabham.

WIN NUMBER TWO: Mika Hakkinen won this Grand Prix fair and square ahead of his McLaren team-mate David Coulthard

Racing to Rio

Sao Paulo wasn't the only city in Brazil wanting to host the race, though, and in 1978 those folk from the rival city along the coast at Rio de Janeiro took over, holding the Grand Prix at their Jacarepagua circuit. With two straights joined by several simple corners, it was not as popular as Interlagos – particularly in that first year, when Reutemann from neighbouring Argentina beat Fittipaldi to the chequered flag. After two years back at Interlagos, Jacarepagua regained the Grand Prix and held on to it for nine years, with Alain Prost notching up five wins and Brazilian Piquet claiming two before Interlagos took over again in 1990.

Sadly, Interlagos was to prove unrecognizable on Formula One's return, as it had been chopped to just over half its original length, with many of the faster corners made less challenging or removed altogether.

A lap starts with a steeply dipping left-right chicane that is fine once the race has got into its stride, but it's a nightmare on the opening lap, as the cars attempt to funnel through the corner without contact while simultaneously giving their all to pass the cars ahead of them. This first corner on the first lap is where much of the race's overtaking is done. As a result, there have been some acrobatic shunts there, including a huge one between Gerhard Berger and Michael Andretti in 1993.

The track then climbs through the course of a long, long left-hander on to the long back straight, which sees drivers hit 185mph before the track feeds into a tight left-hander, Descida do Lago. Drivers have to keep an eye out for overtaking down the inside here under braking. There's then the long climb to the fifth-gear Ferra Dura right-hander, and the track starts twisting after a second-gear right-hander tips the track down to another second-gear corner, Pinheirinho, then up to the even tighter Bico de Plato.

Then it's down the hill and up through the gearbox before the last corner, Juncao – out of which drivers hope they can get a good tow up the hill on to the pit straight, and be in a position to make a move into that opening chicane as the drivers attempt to haul their cars down from 190mph.

Senna wins at last

While the changes didn't appeal to the purists, they proved good for the patriotic fans, as after years of disappointment on his home patch Senna finally won the Brazilian Grand Prix in 1991. Unsurprisingly, the crowd went beserk, but it's never been the same there since he died in 1994.

With Michael Schumacher winning at Interlagos in 1994 and 1995, Damon Hill taking the garlands in 1996 and then Jacques Villeneuve doing the same in 1997, it almost seems that whoever wins the Brazilian Grand Prix goes on to become World Champion. Fittingly, Mika Hakkinen dominated proceedings ahead of McLaren team-mate David Coulthard in 1998, as Michael Schumacher had to make do with finishing a further minute back in third place.

IMOLA

ROUND 4   MAY 2, 1999

Imola is a circuit with a dark past, having seen the all-time great Ayrton Senna perish there a day after rookie Roland Ratzenberger met a similar fate in 1994, but it remains a circuit to stir the soul.

San Marino Grand Prix
I M O L A

Imola

May
2

Circuit length: **4.930km**
Race distance: **62 laps**

Rivazza

Variante Bassa

Traguardo

Variante Alta

Tamburello

Acque Minerali

Villeneuve

Piratella

Tosa

T0 Timing sectors

Imola, Italy: 3.063 miles/4.930km; 62 laps. Lap record: Heinz-Harald Frentzen (Williams-Renault), 1m 25.531s, 128.942mph,1997

1998 results
1 David Coulthard — McLaren
2 Michael Schumacher — Ferrari
3 Eddie Irvine — Ferrari
4 Jacques Villeneuve — Williams
5 Heinz-Harald Frentzen — Williams
6 Jean Alesi — Sauber

It may take years for it to move out from the shadow cast in those two dark days in the spring of 1994, but take the physical entity of Imola and it still excites as the tarmac threads along the banks of a river, then twists up and down through a parkland setting. However, the legacy of the tragedies of 1994 is that chicanes have broken the track's flow and taken the magic out of the mixture.

A lap of the circuit starts with a blast past the start/finish line, but the left-hand Tamburello kink where Senna left the track is now chopped and slowed by a chicane that requires the use of second gear rather than sixth... Then it's pedal-to-the-metal down to the Villeneuve corner where

CHOPPED AND CHANGED: A chicane was inserted at Tamburello after Senna's fatal shunt there in 1994

Ratzenberger hit the wall, and this has been kinked and slowed. This has taken the sting out of the entry to Tosa corner, removing one of the best overtaking spots on the calendar where that combination of a long straight

HERO OF THE TRACK

You'd expect the crowds at Imola to take only Italians to their hearts, but in 1983 they fell in love with Frenchman Patrick Tambay, simply because he had filled the place of former hero Gilles Villeneuve after he died in 1982, and then came to Imola a year later and won there. It didn't concern them that Italian Riccardo Patrese crashed his Brabham out of the lead with five laps to go. What mattered was that Gilles's No. 27 Ferrari had won in Italy.

and potential slipstreaming at up to 195mph into a tight corner would see wonderful outbraking manoeuvres.

From the sharp left at Tosa, the track climbs to the left-hander at Piratella that crests the wooded hilltop. Then the track dives down to the Acque Minerali right-hander before climbing again to the chicane at Variante Alta, from where it drops to the level of the startline via the double-apex left-hander called Rivazza, which sees drivers having to slow from 185mph. The last corner, the Variante Bassa, has been made less extreme – this a result of Rubens Barrichello's monster accident there, also in 1994.

A car breaker

Especially with the slowing effect of the recently added chicanes, Imola is a track that cooks a car's brakes, wears out tyres and bursts transmissions, leading to a higher-than-average number of retirements. It's not as fast as it was in those halcyon days before the insertion of the chicanes, and it's lost the best of its rhythm, but overtaking is still a possibility – which is more than can be said of some of the other circuits on the Formula One calendar.

Visit Imola, and you come away in no doubt that only one team counts

as far as the ever-passionate fans are concerned: Ferrari. Indeed, marque founder Enzo Ferrari named the circuit after his son Dino, who died tragically young. And the level of excitement emanating from a scarlet-clad, flag-waving cast of thousands camped on the hillside opposite the Variante Bassa and running up to the pits has to be experienced. It's like the breaking of the sound barrier if a Ferrari tops the timesheets in qualifying or takes the lead. And if a Ferrari were perchance to win there, well…

A second Italian Grand Prix

It feels as though the circuit has held a Grand Prix for ever, but it was only in 1980 that Imola was given the go-ahead. Since 1981 it has held a Grand Prix early in the season, with the Grand Prix at Monza traditionally slated for the tail end of the season. So how come Italy gets two Grands Prix a year, while other countries have to make do with one? The answer is that the race at Imola is known as the San Marino Grand Prix, named after the nearby principality – the one that always get thrashed at football. So maybe we in Britain will be honoured with the Isle of Man Grand Prix at Oulton Park!

Races at Imola are famous for cars expiring, or even running out of fuel in the closing laps – as used to happen when turbocharged engines ruled the roost and no one made fuel stops. However, the circuit is also famous for big shunts, as experienced by Nelson Piquet at Tamburello in 1987 and Gerhard Berger at the same corner two years later. But the darkest day ever for Ferrari fans came in 1991 when Alain Prost spun one of their beloved red cars off on the parade lap, and then team-mate Jean Alesi ran out of road three laps later.

The 1997 race was the best for years, with Jacques Villeneuve, Heinz-Harald Frentzen and Michael Schumacher all leading at various points. Sadly for the *tifosi*, Schumacher nosed his Ferrari ahead for only one lap during the pit stops, and it was Frentzen who took the honours, finally coming good for Williams after a troubled start to his season. David Coulthard won last year, surviving a scare as a plastic bag blocked a radiator and sent his engine temperature soaring, allowing none other than Ferrari's Michael Schumacher to close in.

MONACO

ROUND 5   MAY 16, 1999

Glamorous, with its yachts, casino and jet-set clientele, Monaco is also dangerous and outdated, and should have no place on the Formula One calendar — save to serve the sponsors. But it remains, and the drivers enjoy racing on their own doorsteps, as most live here in tax exile.

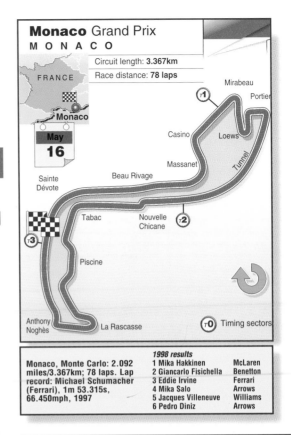

Monaco Grand Prix
M O N A C O

FRANCE

Monaco

May
16

Circuit length: **3.367km**
Race distance: **78 laps**

Mirabeau
Portier
Casino
Loews
Massanet
Tunnel
Beau Rivage
Sainte
Dévote
Tabac
Nouvelle
Chicane
Piscine
Anthony
Noghès
La Rascasse
Timing sectors

Monaco, Monte Carlo: 2.092
miles/3.367km; 78 laps. Lap
record: Michael Schumacher
(Ferrari), 1m 53.315s,
66.450mph, 1997

1998 results	
1 Mika Hakkinen	McLaren
2 Giancarlo Fisichella	Benetton
3 Eddie Irvine	Ferrari
4 Mika Salo	Arrows
5 Jacques Villeneuve	Williams
6 Pedro Diniz	Arrows

A SUPER SETTING: No circuit can match Monaco for a view. This is looking down on Ste Dévote, Tabac and the harbour

Drivers can even hook a wheel over the pavement on the inside of the corner. The Loews hairpin is next; it's not an overtaking place, but every year people try, usually with contact on the exit, such as that between Michael Schumacher and Alexander Wurz there last year.

Then there's the double-right on to the seafront at Portier, the first part of which Michael Schumacher failed to negotiate on the opening lap in 1996. Then comes the tunnel. To make matters trickier, it's not straight, but comprises a long right-hand arc taken at 150mph. Out of the tunnel, blinking in the daylight, drivers hit the anchors and jink left, right, left on to the harbourside. Careering past corpulent yachts and the well-heeled sailors for the weekend, the drivers have to steel themselves for the fast left at Tabac and funnel their cars left, right, right, left around Piscine, and finally jink into the La Rascasse hairpin and get the power down for another lap.

Sponsors love it

The drivers are split as to whether they enjoy it or loathe the thought of being restricted at every move, with pits and paddock crowded in the extreme. Ask the sponsors, though, and they adore the race, as nowhere else on the calendar comes close for the art of networking. It has the harbour, the casino, the beautiful people and its own royal family.

While many races have turned into a procession because overtaking is so tricky, there have been some fantastic Monaco Grands Prix. None more so than in 1982, when three drivers held the lead in the final three-and-a-half laps before Riccardo Patrese recovered from spinning out of the lead to win. There was also Mansell's amazing chase after Senna in 1992, when he did everything but climb over the top of the McLaren in his quest to push his Williams back ahead after an unscheduled pit stop.

The 1997 encounter was also dramatic, as rain swept in and many teams found themselves on the wrong tyres. As expected in rainy conditions, Michael Schumacher dominated for Ferrari for his third Monaco scalp in four years. But the streets were made wetter still by the tears around the Stewart pit, as Rubens Barrichello finished second for not only the team's first points, but its first finish, too.

McLaren returned to the top there last year when Mika Hakkinen was able to win as he pleased once team-mate David Coulthard had retired from his tail, with Giancarlo Fisichella surviving a late-race spin to bring his Benetton home a second ahead of Eddie Irvine's Ferrari.

A moment that will stick in the memory, though, is when Michael Schumacher barged his way past Alexander Wurz's Benetton at Loews, only for the Austrian to repass him at the following corner. Sadly, damage from their impact is probably what caused Wurz's suspension to collapse in the tunnel later in the race, and leave him as a passenger as his car rode the barriers down to the chicane. Mercifully, the gutsy Austrian walked away with no more than a shaking.

SPEED AND POWER: The race week at Monaco is much favoured by the sponsors, but not necessarily teams and drivers

When you compare the wide open spaces of Silverstone or the sweeping majesty of Spa-Francorchamps, the narrow streets used for the Monaco Grand Prix are starkly different in the challenge they offer the drivers. Indeed, three-times World Champion Nelson Piquet once described driving a Formula One car around Monaco as like riding a bicycle around your sitting room: great fun, but it's an accident waiting to happen. And any driver who has raced there has to agree, as the track is twisty, steep and – above all – narrow.

Blink during a lap of Monaco and your car will be in the barriers, which are never far from the racing line.

Precision required

The start is at the curving grid that bends right towards the first corner, the tight right called Ste Devote. If the track were wider, it would be fine, but there's only one line around it, which always leads to trouble at the start as the drivers try to take it two or even three abreast. Or, in the case of Derek Daly in 1980, in the air, as he clipped the car in front, vaulted over it, bounced and then landed on Jean-Pierre Jarier, his Tyrrell team-mate… So caution is required, if rarely applied, here.

Then it's up the hill towards Casino Square, hitting 160mph by the top. The left-hander into Casino Square is blind over a crest, and drivers have to set their cars up unsighted for the right-hander that runs out of the far side of the square and down past the Tip-Top Bar to the Mirabeau hairpin.

HERO OF THE TRACK

Few races have ever become as inextricably linked to one driver as the Monaco Grand Prix did to Graham Hill. During his 18-year Formula One career, the two-times World Champion won the Monaco Grand Prix on five occasions. In the 1960s it became as much a part of the Monaco scenery as Casino Square and the harbourfront to see Hill collecting his trophy from Prince Rainier before heading off for a quick one at the Tip-Top bar. Senna and Schumacher have since shone there.

BARCELONA

ROUND 6 MAY 30, 1999

Barcelona's Catalunya circuit is now well and truly established as the home of the Spanish Grand Prix, after dalliances with the Jarama and Jerez circuits over the past two decades.

Spanish Grand Prix
B A R C E L O N A

Circuit length: 4.727km
Race distance: 65 laps

Barcelona

May
30

La Caixa
Banc Sabadell
Nissan
Campsa
Repsol
Seat
Renault
Elf

Timing sectors

Circuit de Catalunya, Barcelona: 2.937 miles/4.727km; 65 laps. Lap record: Giancarlo Fisichella (Jordan-Peugeot), 1m 22.242s, 128.604mph, 1997

1998 results
1 Mika Hakkinen — McLaren
2 David Coulthard — McLaren
3 Michael Schumacher — Ferrari
4 Alexander Wurz — Benetton
5 Rubens Barrichello — Stewart
6 Jacques Villeneuve — Williams

Spain has never produced a top-line Formula One driver, yet it has a long history of hosting Grands Prix, and five circuits have shared the honour over the years. The first Spanish Grand Prix was held at the round-the-houses Pedralbes circuit on the outskirts of Barcelona back in the early 1950s. However, the country didn't host another Grand Prix until 1968, when the purpose-built Jarama circuit on the outskirts of Madrid took over. Yet Jarama's tenure was short, as a year later the wonderful Montjuich Park circuit in downtown Barcelona took its turn. These two circuits shared the Grand Prix in an alternating pattern that continued until 1975, when the rear wing came off Rolf Stommelen's race-leading Hill chassis, which then vaulted the barrier and killed five spectators. That spelt the end of the scenic and popular Montjuich Park circuit.

Since then, the Spanish Grand Prix has been shared by Barcelona's Catalunya circuit and Jerez, with the balance recently in favour of the former. Jerez is situated at the far end of the country, in the heart of the sherry-producing country south of Seville. Dry and dusty, it's beautifully equipped, but too far from major conurbations to draw large crowds. The track is twisty – especially after the introduction of a chicane following Martin Donnelly's career-ending shunt at the Curva Ferrari behind the pits.

But perhaps in years to come, its principal claim to fame will be that it produced the second closest Grand Prix finish of all time in 1986, when Ayrton Senna's Lotus edged out Nigel Mansell's Williams by 0.014s after almost 200 miles of racing. Or perhaps when it landed an extra race in 1997, hosting the year's final round when the Estoril circuit in neighbouring Portugal failed to complete necessary changes in time. Mika Hakkinen won after being let through on the last lap by new champion Jacques Villeneuve, after the Canadian had survived a title-settling assault by Michael Schumacher.

GOING INTO BATTLE: Eddie Irvine leads from Giancarlo Fisichella as the two competed for fourth place in 1998. Neither driver finished the race

Designed to thrill

However, Barcelona's Catalunya circuit is the nation's true home now. Built at the start of the 1990s, its layout is better than that of other modern circuits in that the designer has taken into account the fact that people like to watch overtaking rather than endless processions, and has designed the circuit so that the lengthy main straight past the pits leads into a sharp right-hand corner approached at 190mph, and thus requires heavy braking. And this is where overtaking happens: under braking after the chasing driver has been able to catch a tow from the car ahead, and been able to slingshot past. And if they get this wrong, there's a massive gravel trap to catch them. A corner like this sorts the men from the boys – especially late in the race when brakes are past their best, making it a contest of bravery as drivers sit it out to see who will be last on to the pedal.

This first corner, Elf, is a right followed by a left, and then there's a long uphill right-hander. Get this right in fifth gear, and a driver will be doing 170mph before hitting the brakes for the Repsol right-hander, from where the track dips and feeds through the Seat left-hander, through a left kink and into the uphill left-hander that takes the cars up to the Campsa corner at the crest of the hill. Then, carrying as much speed as possible over the crest there, drivers hit 180mph down the back straight before the tight left at La Caixa and the start of the climb back up to Banc Sabadell corner. The final two right-handers are crucial to a quick time, as they're fast fifth-gear corners on to the main straight.

Unlucky with rain

Several races through the 1990s have been marked by an unseasonal amount of rain, none more so than in 1996 when Michael Schumacher produced a drive from the top drawer and blitzed the field in his Ferrari as many others failed even to stay on the track, despite circulating at a far more conservative pace as the rain turned torrential.

The 1997 race was marked by heavy tyre wear, with winner Jacques Villeneuve having to nurse his Williams along between its two pit stops for fresh Goodyears, while rival Olivier Panis was able to press far harder on his more resilient Bridgestone rubber as he gave chase en route to second place. Schumacher was in real rubber trouble and had to pit three times on his way to fourth place behind Jean Alesi's Benetton.

Tyres weren't such an issue last year, as the McLarens of Mika Hakkinen and David Coulthard wiped the floor with the opposition. Michael Schumacher, typically the best of the rest, and Benetton's Alexander Wurz were the only other unlapped runners after their respective team-mates, Eddie Irvine and Giancarlo Fisichella, crashed into retirement while contesting fourth place.

HERO OF THE TRACK

With Spanish Formula One fans being desperately short of driving heroes of their own, it's not surprising that they latch on to those who have performed well on their patch. And none has driven better in Spain than Michael Schumacher, who not only walked on water to win in the wet for Ferrari at Barcelona in 1996, but also raced to second place there in 1994 – despite his Benetton being stuck in fifth gear... In short, no one goes better there than him.

MONTREAL

ROUND 7   JUNE 13, 1999

Set on an island in the St Lawrence River in Montreal, the Circuit Gilles Villeneuve looks tame, but it's a car breaker, and every Canadian Grand Prix turns into a battle of attrition.

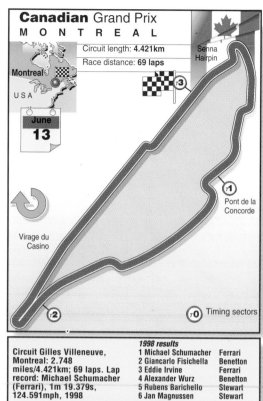

Canadian Grand Prix
M O N T R E A L

Circuit length: **4.421km**
Race distance: **69 laps**

Montreal
USA

June
13

Senna Hairpin

Pont de la Concorde

Virage du Casino

Timing sectors

Circuit Gilles Villeneuve, Montreal: 2.748 miles/4.421km; 69 laps. Lap record: Michael Schumacher (Ferrari), 1m 19.379s, 124.591mph, 1998	*1998 results*	
	1 Michael Schumacher	Ferrari
	2 Giancarlo Fisichella	Benetton
	3 Eddie Irvine	Ferrari
	4 Alexander Wurz	Benetton
	5 Rubens Barichello	Stewart
	6 Jan Magnussen	Stewart

OUT OF THE HAIRPIN: Damon Hill puts the power down at the Pits hairpin, but he retired from third place

If it wasn't for Gilles Villeneuve and, latterly, his son Jacques, Canada would have very little to shout about in Formula One circles. However, Formula One and Canada have been linked in three ways since the country hosted a Grand Prix for the first time in 1967. Firstly, despite no indigenous drivers being regulars on the Formula One scene, there was simply the desire to host a Grand Prix, with local drivers renting cars for their home race.

However, this changed when Gilles Villeneuve rose through from snowmobile racing via the junior formulae to burst on to the international scene in the late 1970s. He pushed Formula One to heights of popularity it had never known, drawing ever more of the Canadian populace away from their more regular interest in ice hockey and, perhaps, snowmobile

racing. Tragically, he died at Zolder in 1982 while trying to qualify his Ferrari for the Belgian Grand Prix, and Canada lost interest again, its new-found race fans looking more to North America's Indycar racing.

It wasn't until the arrival in Formula One of Gilles's son that the third phase of interest was spawned. He warmed his nation up by winning the 1995 Indycar title, and headed for Formula One with Williams. With a strong chance of winning on his home debut in 1996, it seemed that everyone in Quebec wanted to see Jacques win on the circuit named after his late father. He came close, but could do nothing to stop team-mate Damon Hill from winning.

Canada's early Grands Prix were not held in Montreal, but on road circuits up-country at Mosport Park in Ontario and Quebec's Mont Tremblant. These

A CITY BACKDROP: The skyscrapers and one of Montreal's many bridges show the track's city location

races were held in the autumn, and it was a wonder to behold the colour of the leaves on the trees that surrounded both circuits, making the backdrop one of the most attractive in Formula One. With the arrival of Gilles, the Canadians had a front-runner to cheer, and the race was moved to its current Montreal venue, with Gilles winning the first race there in 1978.

A real car breaker

And what a circuit the Circuit Gilles Villeneuve is. Or, more to the point, was – prior to the insertion of chicanes in the early 1990s. The circuit is built on the site of the EXPO '67 display, and it sends car after car into retirement as its bumps and tight corners stress the moving parts like nowhere else. Running around the Olympic rowing basin, and yet pinned in on two sides by the river, there's very little space for the track and even less for the grandstands.

The sprint from the grid to the first corner always sees excited jockeying for position as the track jinks right, goes tight left and then into a right-hand hairpin, the Virage Senna. And, inevitably, someone will get this wrong as the drivers attempt to funnel their cars into an ever-narrowing area. From there, drivers must negotiate a series of esses and chicanes before touching 180mph on the curving back straight – all surrounded by concrete barriers. After yet another chicane comes the Pits Hairpin, the best overtaking spot, where Nigel Mansell waved to the fans on the final lap in 1991, only to stall and let Nelson Piquet through to win… The blast back to the pit straight is taken in sixth, hitting 190mph before the final chicane.

Schumacher's surprise

The 1997 race was even more of a car breaker than usual, with Olivier Panis's Prost sadly hitting the barriers at 150mph, most likely due to a mechanical failure. Panis broke both his legs, and the safety car was

deployed while he was moved to safety. At that same moment, runaway leader David Coulthard stalled in the pits, and this put Michael Schumacher in front to claim a surprise victory when the race was halted four laps later. However, a lot of the fans had already long since left the circuit, as Jacques Villeneuve had lost concentration on the second lap and ended his race against the wall. Typically for Montreal, this didn't make him the first out of the race, as Jan Magnussen, Eddie Irvine and Mika Hakkinen had all beaten him to that distinction…

Last year's action was even more dramatic, as Alexander Wurz was launched over Jean Alesi's Sauber at the start – his Benetton cartwheeling into the huge gravel trap, where it was joined by the entire midfield, necessitating a restart. Then, with the McLarens both hitting mechanical trouble, Michael Schumacher dominated for Ferrari, but only after he'd exited the pits in a rash move that pitched Heinz-Harald Frentzen's Williams off the track.

HERO OF THE TRACK

Gilles Villeneuve remains the most revered driver in modern history – more so even than the late Ayrton Senna. To most, Gilles was a genius at the wheel; a flawed genius, perhaps, but his sideways style never failed to entertain, although some of this was due to his Ferrari's handling inadequacies. Never a World Champion, Gilles won six Grands Prix, and none was as popular as when he won the first Grand Prix in Montreal. No wonder the circuit was named after him…

MAGNY-COURS

Magny-Cours is a very modern circuit in that it is beautifully equipped, but when designing it they forgot to insert any soul; thus it is nobody's favourite place at which to go racing.

TRACK HERO

Alain Prost is by far France's greatest racing driver. Not only did he win four World titles – in 1985, 1986 and 1989 for McLaren, and in 1993 for Williams – but six of his 51 Grand Prix wins came on home ground, firstly at Dijon-Prenois, then four times at Paul Ricard before finally claiming his last two French Grand Prix scalp at Magny-Cours. Nothing would give him greater pleasure than his French charge Olivier Panis winning there this summer.

TWO IN A ROW: Michael Schumacher followed last year's Canadian GP success with a victory at Magny-Cours

While Britain is the home of world motorsport – the centre of excellence not just for Formula One, but also for Indycars, touring cars and even the cars that contest the World Rally Championship – it is France that has the longest history, having been home to the first-ever motor race. That was back in 1894, when a race was held along the public roads from Paris to Rouen. With marques such as Bugatti, Delage, Talbot and Gordini to the fore, France was a major player until the Second World War, after which the Italians took over, then the Germans and then the British in the 1960s.

Six circuits hosted the French Grand Prix before it moved to Magny-Cours, but they now all lag behind modern-day Formula One requirements – rather like Brands Hatch has in England. Lose your Grand Prix, and you lose the revenue to keep up with developments.

A race on the move

Reims was the first French venue to hold a modern day (post-1950) Grand Prix on an almost triangular course of public roads, with its races famed for drivers hunting as a pack as they used each other's slipstreams to haul themselves on to the tail of the car ahead. Interspersed in the same period from the early 1950s to the late 1960s, a trickier track through the trees just outside Rouen was used, complete with a cobbled hairpin…

However, perhaps the greatest track to have hosted the French Grand Prix was used next, high on the hill above Clermont-Ferrand. Dipping and twisting through fast and often blind corners, it was a classic. But its perils had to be faced and, as the cars became ever faster and the drivers decided that they would like to live to see another Christmas, the circuit was judged to be too dangerous. So the flat and fast Paul Ricard circuit just behind the Riviera took over in 1971, with the Grand Prix staying there through the 1980s, with occasional forays to the tighter and hillier – but equally popular – Dijon-Prenois circuit, before Magny-Cours began its reign.

In the days when Paul Ricard and Dijon-Prenois shared the Grand Prix, Magny-Cours was no more than a club circuit. But it had the good fortune to be located in a poor and backward rural area. President Mitterand decided it should be transformed into the centre of technical excellence for French motorsport to help bring some wealth into the region. Despite no one wanting to go there, it has been the home of the French Grand Prix ever since, and it now houses some of France's top teams on its adjacent industrial estate.

A flying start

The best part of the lap at Magny-Cours comes right at the start, with the combination of the tightening 160mph Grande Courbe left-hander flowing into the long, long Estoril right-hander. And it's essential to get this right for a quick exit on to the back straight, as this leads into the principal overtaking point on the whole track: the Adelaide hairpin at the top of the hill, into which the drivers have to drop from 180mph to 35mph. After this ultra-tight right-hander, the track twists down through the Nurburgring 'ess'. Then it's uphill through the fast Imola 'ess' into the Château d'Eau right-hander and the drop down to the track's tightest chicane before the final corner. This is where Jacques Villeneuve spun on the last lap in 1997 while trying to wrest third place from Eddie Irvine. Then, out of this chicane, there's the tight Lycée right-hander on to the pit straight that sees so many drivers all but kiss the pit wall as they get the power down on the exit.

The 1997 race was notable for a German clean sweep of the front, with Michael Schumacher taking pole ahead of Heinz-Harald Frentzen and brother Ralf. Ralf dropped back to sixth and Michael led Heinz-Harald home in an otherwise processional race.

Last year was expected to be a McLaren cake-walk, but the lack of high-

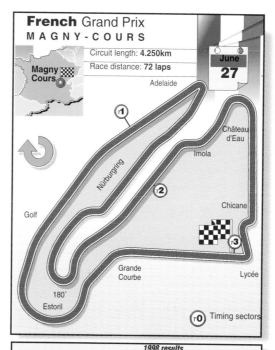

French Grand Prix
MAGNY-COURS

Circuit length: 4.250km
Race distance: 72 laps

June 27

Magny-Cours: 2.641 miles/4.250km; 72 laps. Lap record: David Coulthard (McLaren), 1m 17.523s, 123.355mph, 1998	1998 results	
	1 Michael Schumacher	Ferrari
	2 Eddie Irvine	Ferrari
	3 Mika Hakkinen	McLaren
	4 Jacques Villeneuve	Williams
	5 Alexander Wurz	Benetton
	6 David Coulthard	McLaren

speed corners saw Michael Schumacher qualifying on the front row alongside Mika Hakkinen, and taking the lead when the race was restarted after an aborted first attempt. And team-mate Irvine shot through into second, letting his team leader escape as he held up the McLaren men. Hakkinen spun at the Lycée bend just after passing Irvine, thus falling back again, while David Coulthard hit refuelling problems and had to press hard for the final point-scoring place after coming in for two extra pit stops.

RACING IN THE COUNTRY: The circuit's rural setting is obvious as one looks back down from the Adelaide hairpin

SILVERSTONE

KNOW THE TRACKS

82

ROUND 9   JULY 11, 1999

Silverstone is not only the home of British motor racing, but part of Formula One folklore as the circuit that hosted the first World Championship Grand Prix in 1950, since when it has never looked back.

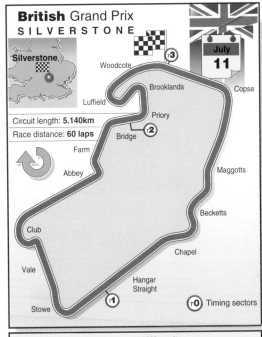

British Grand Prix
S I L V E R S T O N E

Silverstone

Woodcote

Brooklands

Copse

Luffield

Priory

Circuit length: **5.140km**
Race distance: **60 laps**

Bridge

Farm

Maggotts

Abbey

Becketts

Club

Chapel

Vale

Hangar Straight

Stowe

Timing sectors

July 11

Silverstone: 3.194 miles/5.140km; 60 laps. Lap record: Michael Schumacher (Ferrari), 1m 24.475s, 136.115mph, 1997

1998 results	
1 Michael Schumacher	Ferrari
2 Mika Hakkinen	McLaren
3 Eddie Irvine	Ferrari
4 Alexander Wurz	Benetton
5 Giancarlo Fisichella	Benetton
6 Ralf Schumacher	Jordan

SLOWING IT DOWN: The safety car was deployed mid-race last year because of torrential rain

British fans are renowned as the most knowledgeable in the world, but that's not surprising as they have the greatest choice of circuits populated by the fullest array of national formulae, and there's racing every weekend between March and October at which they can see the stars of the future. Best of these is Silverstone, one of the cradles of world motor sport.

Formula One was very different when Silverstone hosted the first modern-day Grand Prix in 1950. On that day, as inaugural World Champion Giuseppe Farina did battle with his Alfa Romeo team-mate Juan-Manuel Fangio, the corners were marked out by oil drums on this otherwise featureless landscape.

Writing about the British Grand Prix and mentioning only Silverstone

is misleading, though, as the race was held at Donington Park in the 1930s – when Mercedes and Auto Union wiped the floor with the British 'opposition'. Formula One took off in the years that followed, with the British trying all they knew to break the Italian/German stranglehold, as Alfa Romeo's domination was followed by Ferrari and Mercedes controlling the game. However, when the first British win came in 1955, it was not in a British car, but a Mercedes, and not at Silverstone but at Aintree – the home of the Grand National horse race. The track ran around the perimeter, and the grandstands were packed when Stirling Moss pipped team-mate Fangio.

The race alternated between Aintree and Silverstone until 1962, when Aintree hosted the race for the second year on the trot. But Brands Hatch

took over, alternating with Silverstone in 1964. However, Brands Hatch lost the battle to host the race after 1986, and is in no state to welcome Formula One back unless major safety work is undertaken. This is a shame, as it produced some cracking races in a natural amphitheatre, such as the one in 1985 when it was masquerading as the Grand Prix of Europe so that Britain could host two Grands Prix that year, and Nigel Mansell scored his first Grand Prix victory.

Some epic duels

The first race of Silverstone's uninterrupted run was in 1987, and it's one that readily springs to mind for its duel between Nigel Mansell and Williams team-mate Nelson Piquet when they ran wheel-to-wheel down the Hangar Straight, their undertrays sparking. The cheer that rang out when the local hero passed the Brazilian into Stowe had to be heard to be believed. Six years later, there was a scrap between Damon Hill and Williams team-leader Alain Prost: just when it looked as though Damon was heading for his first win, his engine blew. Then there was a great race in 1997, with Mika Hakkinen set for his first win until his McLaren's engine blew, handing victory to Jacques Villeneuve.

Last year's race will rank as one of the most confusing, with heavy rain making it difficult for everyone. It also brought out the safety car when aquaplaning became prevalent, wiping out Hakkinen's half-minute lead. Then it ended in confusion when new leader Michael Schumacher was penalized for overtaking under waved yellows, and chose to call in for his stop/go penalty *after* the finish. Amazingly, he was allowed to keep his win…

A changing feast

Chopped to a 100mph bend after Ayrton Senna's death, Copse has since been opened out and is now taken at around 140mph in fourth gear before the drivers grab sixth and hit 185mph as they jink through Maggotts and dive into the Becketts 'esses'". This is the most exhilarating part, as it's taken at 115mph and yet offers a constant change of direction as it dives right, flicks left and then right again. Then it's hard on the power through the Chapel kink and on to the Hangar Straight and up to 190mph before hauling the car down to 105mph so the driver can turn in to the Vale dip after Stowe. Hard left at the end of this, then right through the double-apex Club corner and up to 170mph before the Abbey chicane. Once the fastest corner, this now slows drivers before they reach Bridge, which remains a daunting corner as the cars dive into a dip at 155mph and then turn hard right, firing up into the 'infield section'. This part of the circuit gives a good opportunity to gauge how close cars are to each other as the track meanders in front of the grandstands. Left at Priory, left at Brooklands, then right through Luffield and once more through Woodcote and the lap is complete. It doesn't flow as it used to, but the circuit owners are doing their best to give it back some of its old rhythm.

HERO OF THE TRACK

No British driver has ever whipped a home crowd into a frenzy in the manner Nigel Mansell achieved in the late 1980s when he was always a pace-setter for Williams. He attracted a new breed of fan to Silverstone that had eyes only for him. When they stormed the circuit on the slowing-down lap in 1992, with no regard for the other cars, it was clear that Mansell-mania had gone too far, but he remained a promoter's dream, a driver who would never fail to entertain.

A1-RING

ROUND 10   JULY 25, 1999

The A1-Ring was built over parts of the popular but outdated Osterreichring. Sadly, the best parts were left out, but the tighter new parts certainly provide entertainment, as shown in 1998.

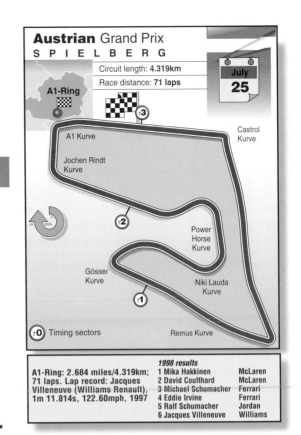

Austrian Grand Prix
S P I E L B E R G

A1-Ring

Circuit length: **4.319km**
Race distance: **71 laps**

July
25

A1 Kurve

Jochen Rindt Kurve

Castrol Kurve

Power Horse Kurve

Gösser Kurve

Niki Lauda Kurve

Remus Kurve

Timing sectors

A1-Ring: 2.684 miles/4.319km; 71 laps. Lap record: Jacques Villeneuve (Williams Renault), 1m 11.814s, 122.60mph, 1997

1998 results
1	Mika Hakkinen	McLaren
2	David Coulthard	McLaren
3	Michael Schumacher	Ferrari
4	Eddie Irvine	Ferrari
5	Ralf Schumacher	Jordan
6	Jacques Villeneuve	Williams

UP, UP AND AWAY: The climb to the A1-Ring's first corner is one of the steepest in Formula One

HERO OF THE TRACK

Niki Lauda was 'Mr Motor Racing' in the 1970s. Initially dismissed as simply a driver with money, Niki soon impressed and landed a Ferrari drive. The team was in turmoil, but he turned it around and won the 1975 and 1977 titles before joining Brabham. He quit for three years to set up his airline, then came back to Formula One by joining McLaren in 1982, winning a third World Championship title in 1984. That year, he won on home ground at his tenth attempt.

HIS LAST HOME SHOW: Gerhard Berger in his Benetton-Renault, making his last Austrian Grand Prix appearance in 1997

The Osterreichring was one of the world's great circuits. Indeed, in the 1970s it vied with Spa-Francorchamps for the mantle of being the world's greatest circuit. Not only was it popular with the drivers, but the spectators too, as shown in 1982 when Elio de Angelis's Lotus was pushed all the way to the finish line by Keke Rosberg's Williams, with Elio holding on to win by just 0.05 seconds, the third-smallest margin ever. It is said that an elderly journalist stayed away in 1997 rather than attend the first Austrian Grand Prix held on the A1-Ring. Drastic action, certainly, but it gives a clue to the anger that many traditionalists felt about the transformation.

However, the creation of the A1-Ring was merely a way of ensuring that the circuit was accepted by the sport's governing body and thus welcomed back on to the Grand Prix calendar after a ten-year break.

Only the vague outline of the Osterreichring has been retained. In essence, the fast sweepers have been truncated or bypassed, and there has also been the unforgivable insertion of three second-gear corners. Thank goodness the Styrian mountain scenery remains as glorious as before.

It has taken the people behind the A1-Ring years of campaigning to land the financial backing required to modernize the circuit to a point where it could host a Grand Prix again. Fittingly, this second generation of Austrian Grands Prix is kicking off just as Austria's next rising star, Alexander Wurz, is making his first strides in Formula One. This year, he

is starting his second full season with Benetton after his hugely impressive three-race trial in 1997 was followed by some strong displays in 1998 – much to the delight of Austrian race fans, who were brought up on the exploits of Jochen Rindt, Niki Lauda and Gerhard Berger.

First-time winners

As well as the return of an Austrian Grand Prix being exciting news for Austria's race fans, it's also good news for those who can remember back to the 1970s when the race had a habit of producing first-time winners, with Vittorio Brambilla, John Watson and Alan Jones doing so in consecutive years between 1975 and 1977. Brambilla's surprise success in 1975 remains the most memorable of these as a deluge turned the race into a lottery, and through the murk came the unfancied Italian in his orange March. Disproving the theory that he would be one of the likely candidates to crash out in the conditions, he was still in front when the race was stopped early, and so happy was he at seeing the chequered flag that he got over-excited on the slowing-down lap and crashed his car…

However, that old tradition of producing first-time winners almost returned first time out, with Formula One rookie Jarno Trulli looking set for victory for the new Prost team in 1997 until he emerged from his first pit stop just behind Jacques Villeneuve's Williams and then had his engine blow. Maybe some things have been passed down from the Osterreichring after all…

Last year's race was a McLaren one-two, even though David Coulthard had to fight his way from the back to second, after being pitched into a spin on the opening lap and having to pit for a new nose. Michael Schumacher recovered from having to pit to repair the damage done by a huge airborne moment between the two parts of the final corner, and was able to grab third from Eddie Irvine when his team-mate surprisingly had to slow with 'brake problems'.

Not what it used to be

A lap of the A1-Ring sees the cars climbing steeply from the grid at 180mph up and over a brow to the first corner, but this comes earlier on the A1-Ring than on its predecessor, the right-hander being situated some 200 metres before the old Hella Licht chicane. And it's certainly no sweeper, being taken at 45mph in second gear… Then there's a long climb to the Remus Kurve, now a second-gear hairpin with a steeply climbing entry that's also approached at 180mph. Exiting the corner, the drivers blast up to 180mph again as they descend to the Gosser Kurve, a third-gear double-apex right-hander in place of the faster Boschkurve of old. The track doubles across the face of the slope for a pair of left-handers which take the track back behind the pits and fire the cars up a hill towards the final corner: the Rindt Kurve. This is now a testing right-hander followed by a tighter right on to the start/finish straight.

HOCKENHEIM

ROUND 11   AUGUST 1, 1999

Hockenheim is a combination of flat-out straights, simple chicanes and a stadium section in which 150,000 German fans can wave their flags and shout for their hero, Michael Schumacher.

German Grand Prix
H O C K E N H E I M

Hockenheimring

Circuit length: **6.823km**
Race distance: **45 laps**

August
1

Jim Clark Kurve

Ostkurve

Ayrton Senna Kurve

Nordkurve

Sachs

Agip Kurve

Südkurve

Timing sectors

Hockenheim: 4.239 miles/6.823km; 45 laps. Lap record: Gerhard Berger (Benetton-Renault), 1m 45.747s, 144.337mph, 1997

1998 results	
1 Mika Hakkinen	McLaren
2 David Coulthard	McLaren
3 Jacques Villeneuve	Williams
4 Damon Hill	Jordan
5 Michael Schumacher	Ferrari
6 Ralf Schumacher	Jordan

The German Grand Prix hasn't always been held at Hockenheim, though. Indeed, with only two exceptions, it was held at the Nurburgring from 1951 to 1976, and the Nurburgring is a track that still makes older fans dewy-eyed. At over 14 miles in length, it offered more than a hundred corners, with points where the cars would become airborne and others where they would have to fight to stay within the confines of banked corners. Sadly, fans and drivers were shaken out of their reverie when Niki Lauda nearly lost his life there in 1976. Spectacular, yes, safe, no…

THE MCLARENS TO THE FRONT: Lights out and time to go as the McLaren men leave the grid for another one-two

The two years during that period when the race went elsewhere were 1959 – when it was held at the Avus circuit in Berlin, where two banked corners were joined by two enormously long straights – and 1970, when it had its first foray to Hockenheim. This was a circuit that was little liked, as no one close to the heart of the sport could forget the fact that it had claimed the life of one of the all-time greats. Jimmy Clark died there in an inconsequential Formula Two race at the start of 1968, shortly after he'd clinched his 25th Grand Prix win for Lotus. Something had broken, it seems, and he was pitched into the trees.

Then in 1977 the German Grand Prix came to Hockenheim for good, as the Nurburgring was consigned to lower levels of racing. Fortunately, with every passing year, the memory of Clark recedes slightly, and another layer of veneer is put down to give the track a happier history. There have been some great races there, too – exciting slipstreaming affairs with furious ducking and diving as the pack splits up at the chicanes and those at the rear try to slingshot past their opponents. And the huge grandstands have been packed every year since, with the exception of 1985, when the Grand Prix returned to the Nurburgring. Not to the Nordschleife, though, but to a modern circuit built around the old pits. With its constant-radius corners and grandstands set back a long way from the track behind huge gravel traps and even larger grass verges, the circuit lost its atmosphere.

Cheering for 'Schumi'

Michael Schumacher may have been born closer to the Nurburgring, but it's at Hockenheim that the cheering for him is loudest, for it possesses the best arena in modern-day Formula One, with 150,000 people packed into the grandstands in the 'stadium' section. When they cheer, the drivers can hear them over their engine noise. It's impressive, but can also be daunting if your name is Damon Hill and you are attempting to stand in the way of Michael Schumacher's bid for another world title. Sadly, in 1995 death threats were even issued to Hill by some of these 'patriots'.

Hockenheim has been a happy hunting ground for Gerhard Berger, though. In 1994 he ended Ferrari's longest run without a win. Then in 1996

he was set to put Benetton back at the front after a barren spell since Michael Schumacher left the team, when his engine blew with three laps to go. In 1997, he came back from illness, his father's death and the news that he had no future with Benetton to start on pole, set fastest lap and win.

The home fans were distraught last year when Michael Schumacher had his worst run of the season, his Ferrari unusually off the pace as Mika Hakkinen and David Coulthard powered into the distance in their McLarens. Schumacher finished fifth, behind the improving Williams and Jordan of Jacques Villeneuve and Damon Hill, respectively.

Town and country

Hockenheim falls into two parts: the 'stadium' and the 'country', one part tight and twisty, the other flat-out straights broken by three chicanes. The first corner is a fourth-gear right-hander, where Damon Hill fell off when leading on to the second lap in 1995. Then it's a blast up to the first chicane, the Jim Clark Kurve, hitting 205mph. A second-gear right and a left, and it's back up to 200mph to the far end of the loop and the Ost Kurve chicane. Then an arcing right on to another straight down to the third chicane. Known as the Ayrton Senna Kurve, this differs in that it's left then right. The cars remain out of sight until they burst back out of the trees at Agip Kurve and arrive back into the infield. Some passing moves are pulled off at Agip, but many prefer to dive past into the left-handed second-gear Sachs Kurve. There's a kink, and then a double-apex third-gear right on to the start/finish straight.

HUNGARORING

ROUND 12   AUGUST 15, 1999

Hungary was on the other side of the Iron Cutrain when it landed a Grand Prix in 1986, but time moved on and so did politics, and now the Hungaroring is an established venue offering some great viewing.

Hungarian Grand Prix
H U N G A R O R I N G

Circuit length: **3.968km**
Race distance: **77 laps**

August
15

Budapest

0 = Turn number

7 0   Timing sectors

Hungaroring: 2.465 miles/3.968km; 77 laps.
Lap record: Nigel Mansell (Williams-Renault), 1m 18.308s, 113.349mph, 1992

1998 results
1 Michael Schumacher   Ferrari
2 David Coulthard   McLaren
3 Jacques Villeneuve   Williams
4 Damon Hill   Jordan
5 Heinz-Harald Frentzen   Williams
6 Mika Hakkinen   McLaren

MICHAEL'S MASTERCLASS: Schumacher didn't have the best car in 1998, but he did have the best tactics

Back in the 1970s, the thought of a Grand Prix taking place in an Eastern European country such as Hungary would have been as likely to come true as pigs are to fly. However, with the politics of the region changing as communism retreated and the Iron Curtain was breached, Hungary had its Grand Prix by 1986. That first race saw Nelson Piquet win for Williams ahead of Ayrton Senna's Lotus, with the rest all a lap and more behind. Two years later, Senna hit the top spot, finishing half a second ahead of McLaren team-mate Alain Prost.

In the race's short history, the Hungaroring has also been the scene of Nigel Mansell clinching the World Championship in 1992 by finishing second behind Ayrton Senna, and Damon Hill scoring his first Grand Prix win just 12 months later. Then, of course, Hill nearly won there for a third time in 1997, albeit this time in an Arrows rather than a Williams. His performance rocked the form books, from qualifying third to hunting down and passing Michael Schumacher's Ferrari for the lead, to pulling clear and dominating proceedings as his Bridgestone tyres worked

supremely in the summer heat. But then it all went wrong with three laps
to go and his gearbox started to pack up. Every British Formula One fan
will have ridden those final three laps with Damon, as he went slower and
slower and former Williams team-mate Jacques Villeneuve got closer and
closer, ran on the dirt and passed him halfway around the final lap. Still,
second place was far more than even Hill could have dreamed of.

But perhaps the greatest showing there came last year when Ferrari
technical brain Ross Brawn masterminded Michael Schumacher's victory
over the superior McLarens by putting the German on to a three-stop
strategy. It was a close-run thing, but it worked and counted for double
as title rival Mika Hakkinen faltered with a suspension problem and could
finish only sixth.

Fantastic viewing opportunities

The hills outside Hungary's capital, Budapest, are gently rolling. This
provides the terrain for a circuit that offers better viewing potential than
any since Brands Hatch disappeared from the Formula One calendar at the
end of 1986. The Kent circuit was adored by spectators for the way in
which its natural amphitheatre provided them with a good view of a large
proportion of each lap.

The Hungaroring makes the most of the natural terrain in that it spans
both sides of a wooded valley and the dip in between, offering fantastic
views from almost every vantage point.

The start/finish straight sits high on one of the two side-slopes,
towered over by a natural grandstand that runs its length, with the track at
the same level as the track on the opposite side of the valley. This straight
feeds into a tight right-hander that dips from entry to exit as it turns back
on itself. A downhill left-hander comes next, before a dipping right-hander
that feeds the drivers on to a straight that drops to the bottom of the
valley, with cars hitting 160mph before climbing up the other side and

HERO OF THE TRACK

Damon Hill has every reason to like the Hungaroring, as it
was here that he scored his first Grand Prix win, for Williams
in 1993. It was here, too, that he put his championship
challenge back on track in 1995 by dominating as rival
Michael Schumacher faltered. Then, in 1997, he nearly
pulled off the surprise of the decade when he came within a
lap of winning for Arrows before his gearbox packed up and
he fell back to second. Arrows has never gone as well since.

kinking left. The right-hander at the top puts the cars into a twisty section
as the track jinks right and left until it reaches Turn Eleven and drops to
the right and down to Turn Ten. From here, it climbs all the way up through
to the final corner, a long third-gear right-hander that opens on to the main
straight. A good exit speed is necessary if a driver wants to get into the
slipstream of the car ahead down the straight at up to 175mph for a
potential passing move into the first corner.

Where to pass

With a track this tight, twisty and bumpy, there are few obvious overtaking
places, with passing most likely during the many pit stops necessitated
by the circuit's abrasive, tyre-destroying surface. Indeed, the run down
to the first corner offers the only obvious passing opportunity, as long
as the following driver can get enough of a tow to slingshot past into the
braking zone. The drivers, however, reckon that the circuit's low-speed
nature means that they can have a stab at passing at numerous points
without taking too much of a risk. What they do have to watch out for,
though, is heat exhaustion, as this land-locked country can be
sweltering at the time of its Grand Prix slot in August, with huge
electrical storms bursting overhead.

SPA-FRANCORCHAMPS

ROUND 13   AUGUST 29, 1999

For many fans, no year is complete without a pilgrimage to Spa-Francorchamps. The famous chips and mayonnaise are fantastic, but its appeal is that it's the greatest racing circuit in the world.

Situated among the forests in the Ardennes hills in eastern Belgium, on the edge of the village of Francorchamps a few miles up the hill from the spa town of Spa, the circuit is blessed with challenging terrain plus a handful of the world's leading corners. For all this eulogy, the current circuit isn't a patch on the original. That was mighty, but its safety was less than adequate, as Jackie Stewart discovered when he found himself trapped in his upturned car soaked in petrol after crashing in 1966. And this triggered him to lead a crusade for greater driver safety.

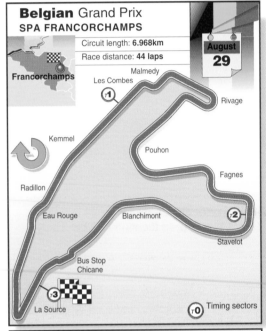

Belgian Grand Prix
SPA FRANCORCHAMPS

Circuit length: 6.968km

Race distance: 44 laps

August 29

Francorchamps

Malmedy
Les Combes
Rivage
Kemmel
Pouhon
Radillon
Fagnes
Eau Rouge
Blanchimont
Stavelot
Bus Stop Chicane
La Source
Timing sectors

Spa-Francorchamps: 4.350 miles/6.968km; 44 laps. Lap record: Alain Prost (Williams-Renault), 1m 51.095s, 140.424mph, 1993

1998 results
1 Damon Hill   Jordan
2 Ralf Schumacher   Jordan
3 Jean Alesi   Sauber
4 Heinz-Harald Frentzen Williams
5 Pedro Diniz   Arrows
6 Jarno Trulli   Prost

HOLD YOUR BREATH: Eau Rouge is hard enough in the dry, but in the wet it's a real focus for a driver's mind...

The track used to be almost twice the length as it dived into the next valley towards Malmedy before rejoining the current track on the climb up from Stavelot. It was frighteningly fast, and there was nothing to stop cars from taking to the trees along its edge. Sadly, it claimed more than its share of fatalities, including British drivers Chris Bristow and Alan Stacey in 1960. Their contemporary, and later double World Champion, Jim Clark didn't mind admitting that he loathed the place, even though he won there four times. To make matters even more risky, the weather in the Ardennes is fickle, and there would often be rain falling heavily at one end of the track and not at the other…

The world's greatest corner

A lap begins with a sprint uphill past the end of the pits to the La Source hairpin, scene of much wheel-banging at the start. Luckily it's wide on the exit, allowing a variety of lines as the track plunges downhill past the old pits and grandstands to Eau Rouge. And it truly is the mother and father of corners as the downhill slope changes immediately into a steep ascent, with a left-right 'ess' thrown in for good measure, all taken in sixth gear at 180mph. Then, with the driver still suffering from compression, the track crests the slope and immediately bends left. There have been some major accidents as drivers have got it wrong, such as Alessandro Zanardi when he dropped his Lotus in 1993 and then Jacques Villeneuve last year. It's crucial to get a good run through Eau Rouge, for it's followed by a long straight up to the 'esses' at Les Combes, which are a favourite overtaking place for those who managed to get a tow and slingshot past on the approach to the braking area at 190mph.

The track cuts away from the course of the original circuit and dips to the Rivage hairpin before diving through a left-handed kink and then on down to the off-camber double-apex left-hander at Pouhon that's taken at around 150mph. Next up are the Fagnes sweepers, which take the track to its lowest point where it rejoins the original circuit then climbs up through the flat-out left at Blanchimont. The track has just one more trick up its sleeve: the Bus Stop chicane, where drivers often try and overtake on the way in, using all the kerbs and more.

A country divided

For all the merits of Spa-Francorchamps, it hasn't always been the home of the Belgian GP, as Belgians are either Flems from the coastal end of the country or French-speaking Walloons from the end that contains Spa-Francorchamps. Thus the race was given to the Flems in the early 1970s, when it was held twice at Nivelles near Brussels and then more frequently at Zolder to the north-west of Liege. But Zolder claimed the life of Gilles Villeneuve in 1982. The race returned to Spa-Francorchamps in 1983, was held at Zolder one last time in 1984, but has remained at Spa ever since.

Ayrton Senna provided one of the best memories by lapping as fast on slicks in the rain as most front-runners could manage on treaded tyres in 1992. Following Senna's death at Imola in 1994, Eau Rouge was modified. Since scoring his first win there in 1993, Michael Schumacher has continued to be the man to beat at Spa-Francorchamps, and his drive to victory in 1997 emphasized his genius as he alone sussed the changing weather before the start and raced clear as it rained. He looked to have done the same again in the wet last year, but he hit David Coulthard when the McLaren driver slowed to let himself be lapped. So the race went to Damon Hill, giving Jordan its first win ahead of team-mate Ralf Schumacher. However, the image that will remain is the massive first-lap accident triggered by Coulthard on the hill down from La Source to Eau Rouge that involved 13 cars; amazingly there wasn't a single serious injury, but the incident left a scene that looked as though a bomb had gone off. Unsurprisingly, the race had to be restarted.

HERO OF THE TRACK

Belgium's greatest driver was Jacky Ickx, a former motorcycle trials champion who had class written all over him when he converted to racing cars in the 1960s. He was never more sublime than in the wet, something that is always useful at Spa. Ironically, he never won at his home circuit, but he did win elsewhere eight times, and was pipped to the 1970 title by Jochen Rindt when racing for Ferrari. He also won the Le Mans 24 Hours a record six times.

MONZA

ROUND 14   SEPTEMBER 12, 1999

You had only to observe the unparalleled joy that overflowed last September when the Ferraris of Schumacher and Irvine finished first and second to understand why Monza is a temple of Formula One.

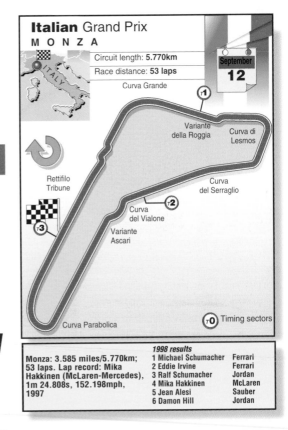

Italian Grand Prix
M O N Z A

Circuit length: 5.770km
Race distance: 53 laps

September 12

Curva Grande
Variante della Roggia
Curva di Lesmos
Rettifilo Tribune
Curva del Serraglio
Curva del Vialone
Variante Ascari
Curva Parabolica
Timing sectors

Monza: 3.585 miles/5.770km; 53 laps. Lap record: Mika Hakkinen (McLaren-Mercedes), 1m 24.808s, 152.198mph, 1997

1998 results

1 Michael Schumacher	Ferrari
2 Eddie Irvine	Ferrari
3 Ralf Schumacher	Jordan
4 Mika Hakkinen	McLaren
5 Jean Alesi	Sauber
6 Damon Hill	Jordan

Walk along the wide straight past the pits at Monza towards the first chicane, and you will catch sight of a piece of track that has long been abandoned. You can guess why, as it's so steeply banked that it would scare even the Indycar racers of today who ply their trade on America's ovals. But this banking made up 180-degree bends at either end of a road course that was built in a park near Milan in 1922, when it also offered a road course and many combinations of the two. Amazingly, the banked corners were used until 1961.

When it comes to the great Formula One circuits of the past, Monza, Silverstone, the Nurburgring and Spa-Francorchamps stand out. They're all still with us, too, although safety requirements have demanded that they should be chopped and changed to ensure a bloodbath is avoided. Yet, for all the modifications, Monza remains a wonderful place.

Spoiling the curves

While the shape of today's circuit is not dissimilar to the original road course, its flow has been changed by the insertion of chicanes in 1972 to check the escalating speed of the cars. The first of these chicanes is reached on the long run to the first corner, the right-hand Curva Grande. Even so, Formula One cars still take this corner in fifth gear at around 175mph. Without the chicane, the mind boggles at what speeds would be seen.

There's then a straight up to the Lesmos, but in 1976 a chicane called the Curva della Roggia was inserted. However, even with this, the two Lesmo right-handers are exciting enough to keep adrenaline pumping. The Lesmos were made tighter in 1994 as part of the post-Senna safety campaign. Then the cars fire off down a straight, going under the old banked circuit and into the Variante Ascari, the relatively fast third chicane inserted where a wicked left-hander used to lurk. Next up is a 200mph straight before the Parabolica which spits the cars on to the main straight.

HARD ON THE BRAKES: The once open sweeps of Monza are now interrupted by three chicanes

FORZA FERRARI: Only one team counts for the *tifosi* at Monza and it's the one with the red cars

It's inevitable that such a high-speed track produces major accidents – one of which happened in 1990 when Derek Warwick's Lotus came flying out of the Parabolica upside down on the first lap. No sooner had his wreck come to a stop than he scrambled out, ran back to the pits, got in the team's spare car and went out for the restart…

The home of the *tifosi*

To understand the tifosi, the Italian fans, is to understand Monza and its rich history. For their passion for motor racing, for Formula One and for Ferrari in particular, is all-consuming. The fact that they bleed red when cut proves, to them, that they are born Ferrari fans. For a Ferrari to win is paramount and it ranks higher in their esteem even than victory for an Italian driving for another team. So, since he joined Ferrari from Benetton, Michael Schumacher has gone from public enemy to a saint-like standing thanks to turning Ferrari around from extravagant squanderers of Italian taxpayers' money to Grand Prix winners once more.

The lap record is still a whisker under 150mph, but before the chicanes were inserted, whole Grands Prix at Monza were run at that pace, with the fastest ever being in 1971 when Peter Gethin won at a race average of 150.755mph. For the record, that was also the closest Grand Prix finish of all time as his BRM was just 0.01 seconds ahead of Ronnie Peterson's March, with the next three cars home covered by 0.61 seconds after the greatest-ever example of drivers hunting in a slipstreaming pack.

There was a pack hunting for victory again in 1997, running nose-to-tail before David Coulthard won for McLaren by a short nose from Jean Alesi's Benetton and Heinz-Harald Frentzen's Williams. But this was a very different race thanks to the track's current shape, and the Scot only moved from third to first thanks to a slick pit stop. Indeed, there was probably more overtaking on the final lap of the 1971 Italian GP than there was all race in 1997… Mind you, the top five were covered by just six-and-a-half seconds.

However, last year's Ferrari one-two for Schumacher and Eddie Irvine was the race that will be remembered for years to come, as it put Schumacher level on points with McLaren's Mika Hakkinen with two races to go, and moved Ferrari to within 10 points of McLaren in the Constructors' Championship. By rights, the race should have belonged to Coulthard, but his McLaren's engine blew when he was leading and Schumacher took Hakkinen for the lead on the same lap when they were unsighted by smoke from Nakano's blown engine. Hakkinen was closing in again when he spun off and could only limp to the finish as Irvine and Schumacher demoted him to fourth.

HERO OF THE TRACK

One of the greatest heroes of the Monza crowd was Clay Regazzoni from the Italian-speaking sector of Switzerland. However, he was considered as one of their own because he drove a Ferrari, and he did so successfully at a time when the team was at a low ebb. Joining part way through 1970, he did what all Ferrari drivers dream of doing, and won at Monza in his maiden year, a feat he repeated in 1975.

NURBURGRING

Luxembourg Grand Prix
N Ü R B U R G R I N G

Circuit length: **4.556km**
Race distance: **67 laps**

September
26

Nürburgring

ITT-bogen

Veedol-S

Coca-Cola Kurve

Bit- Kurve

RTL Kurve

Castrol-S

Dunlop-Kehre

Ford Kurve

Timing sectors

ROUND 15   SEPTEMBER 26, 1999

Germany's second Grand Prix, at the Nurburgring, used to be called the Luxembourg GP, but this season it has reverted to its previous name, the European GP.

European Grand Prix	1998 results	
Nurburgring, 2.831 miles/4.556km, 67 laps. Lap record: Heinz-Harald Frentzen (Williams-Renault), 1m 18.805s, 129.330mph, 1997	1 Mika Hakkinen	McLaren
	2 Michael Schumacher	Ferrari
	3 David Coulthard	McLaren
	4 Eddie Irvine	Ferrari
	5 Heinz-Harald Frentzen	Williams
	6 Giancarlo Fisichella	Benetton

If you want to know why Germany hosts two Grands Prix every year, look no further than Michael Schumacher. He came along and started winning Grands Prix for Benetton in the early 1990s, and turned Germany overnight into a country that was interested in Formula One as well as in football. Germany had not enjoyed sustained success in modern-day Formula One: its Mercedes had shone in the mid-1950s; Wolfgang von Trips starred but was killed in 1961; Stefan Bellof had done likewise in 1985, until he met a similar end. Then nothing, until Schumacher. And then the blue touch-paper was lit, and everyone wanted to watch Formula One.

With the German Grand Prix at Hockenheim a sell-out, another race was needed. So the Nurburgring circuit, which had held the nominal European Grand Prix in 1984 and the German Grand Prix the year after, was awarded the European Grand Prix again in 1995 and 1996. For 1997, the title of the European Grand Prix was withheld, in case the required safety modifications at Portugal's Estoril circuit were not completed in time and a quick move to Jerez in Spain was needed – this would require the European Grand Prix title, since Spain had already hosted a Grand

RUNNING UP THE HILL: It's a flat-out sprint back up the hill from the hairpin, with a few esses for good luck

Prix. Thus the race at the Nurburgring was renamed the Luxembourg Grand Prix, much like Italy's second race at Imola is named the San Marino Grand Prix. And this is how it stayed last year.

A thorough transformation

The Nurburgring of today can never be mistaken for the circuit that hosted Germany's annual showpiece event between 1951 and 1976. Known as the Nordschleife, the original circuit weighed in at 14 miles, with corners almost too numerous to count. However, the drivers felt it was too dangerous for Formula One when Niki Lauda was nearly killed there in 1976, and it was decided the race should be moved to Hockenheim.

The contemporary circuit was built around the old pits, echoing none of the characteristics of the Nordschleife. Instead of a narrow track winding its way through the trees, the circuit is wide, open and surrounded by gravel traps and grandstands.

Yet, for all the criticism from those who hanker after the Nordschleife, it is not such a bad circuit. It has hosted some great races since 1984, with the race in 1995 standing out as Schumacher tracked down Jean Alesi's Ferrari and then passed it for the lead with just three laps to go, to all but clinch his second title for Benetton. The 1997 race was also a thriller, as Schumacher was knocked off at the first corner by his brother, and the two runaway McLarens both blew up within a lap of each other, handing a soft win to Jacques Villeneuve.

Then last year's race was an epic as Mika Hakkinen fought his way from behind Schumacher to win a straight fight that gave him a four-point lead going into the championship finale.

The lie of the land

The Nurburgring's first corner seldom fails to entertain. It's a right-hander approached in sixth gear at around 170mph, and drivers need to haul their cars down to 90mph to get around it. Many fail, especially on the first lap as they try to funnel their cars on to a narrow racing line, and several invariably end up in the huge gravel trap, out of which some are able to emerge.

Next up is a sweeping left-hander, after which it's downhill through a left, a tighter right and then a second-gear, right-hand hairpin. It's uphill out of here, with flat-out acceleration up to a left-right ess and then the Sachskurve. This is the third-gear left-hander out of which Damon Hill crashed in 1995 to effectively hand the title to Schumacher.

The track dips through the right-hand Bitkurve, a sixth-gear kink, and then rises again to the tight Veedol chicane where Schumacher passed Alesi in that same race. Finally, there's the second-gear last corner, out of which drivers look to get into a position to slingshot past the car ahead into the first corner.

HERO OF THE TRACK

Jochen Mass was Germany's main man in the 1970s, but it never quite came right for him. Indeed, he won only one Grand Prix – the Spanish in 1975 – but only half points were awarded, as it had been stopped early by an accident. In 1976 it looked as though he would win at the Nurburgring, having guessed right and fitted slicks, but Niki Lauda's life-threatening accident stopped the race and his advantage was lost. He later quit Formula One and starred on the sportscar scene.

SEPANG

ROUND 16   OCTOBER 17, 1999

Formula One has long been talking of breaking into South-East Asia as restrictions on tobacco sponsorship in Europe have been increased. This is why Malaysia is the latest addition to the Grand Prix calendar.

At first glance, motor racing and Malaysia do not seem to go hand in hand. Yet, for all the apparent lack of history, races have long been held in this tropical country – first, club-level races on temporary street circuits such as Johore Bahru and at Penang, and then more professional races on the purpose-built Shah Alam circuit to the north of the capital, Kuala Lumpur. This was given a huge boost in 1985 when a major sportscar race was held there, with victory going to Jacky Ickx and Jochen Mass in a works Porsche 962. Local touring car and sportscar classes then predominated, but international racing stayed away.

South-East Asia then developed a motor-racing network of its own in the 1990s, with its regional one-make single-seater category, Formula Asia, enjoying good growth, later to be replaced by the Asian Formula 2000 series.

The importance of having a cost-effective training formula has been proved by the development of Alexander Yoong, who graduated to the British Formula Three series last year. Watch out in the future, too, for Ng Wai Leong, who hopes to follow in his wheeltracks.

Touring car racing remains the strongest draw in Malaysia, though,

STATE OF THE ART: The all-new Sepang circuit has been built with the world's most modern racing facilities

WIDE OPEN SPACES: A feature of the Sepang circuit is that the circuit is wide enough to make overtaking possible

with the South-East Asian Touring Car Zone Challenge drawing in entries from Indonesia, Hong Kong and Thailand.

An all-new facility

For all the recent development of Malaysian motorsport, the Sepang circuit near Kuala Lumpur that will host the country's first Grand Prix this October has not been tried by the local heroes. Indeed, it's an all-new track built to an unusual design.

The most marked feature of its design is the massive 30,000-seater grandstand that looks like a lengthy probe, as it not only runs the length of the pit straight, but it also has an equal-sized rear side that overlooks the straight approaching the final corner.

While this double-fronted grandstand houses the vast majority of the spectators, they shouldn't feel that they are missing out on most of the circuit's corners, as Sepang is built on level ground, and thus they can see to the predominantly slow and twisty corners spread on either side that connect these two straights.

The lap begins with a tight right-hand corner, which is effectively a hairpin that feeds back into a left-hand hairpin, rather like a tightened-up version of the first two corners at the Hungaroring. It then feeds off through a long right as the drivers go up through the gears on to a straight that ends with a tight right-hander. A longish left is followed by a more open right and a pair of rights on to a short straight into a tight, left-hand hairpin. This is a possible passing location, but only time will tell.

The lap is completed by a pair of rights and a left before a long right on to the back straight, which takes the drivers up to another left-hand hairpin on to the start/finish straight, with this last corner forming a definite overtaking place. And if a driver fails to get by here, they could always get into position and have a go at slipstreaming the car ahead down the start/finish straight into the first corner.

The South-East Asian economy may have taken a big hit in 1998, but when it turns around, the circuit will be joined on Sepang's Gateway Park complex by bars, restaurants, shops, gyms and even an international airport.

SUZUKA

ROUND 17   OCTOBER 31, 1999

Suzuka is traditionally the venue for the season's final Grand Prix. Michael Schumacher is no doubt hoping that it will treat him better this year, after he lost the title race to Mika Hakkinen there last year.

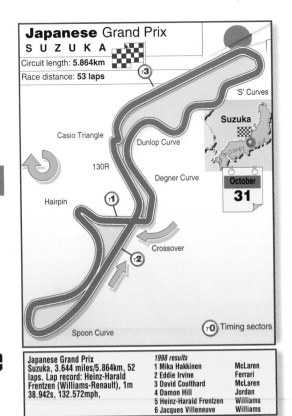

Japanese Grand Prix
S U Z U K A
Circuit length: **5.864km**
Race distance: **53 laps**

'S' Curves

Casio Triangle

Dunlop Curve

Suzuka

130R

Degner Curve

October
31

Hairpin

Crossover

Spoon Curve

Timing sectors

Japanese Grand Prix Suzuka, 3.644 miles/5.864km, 52 laps. Lap record: Heinz-Harald Frentzen (Williams-Renault), 1m 38.942s, 132.572mph,	1998 results	
	1 Mika Hakkinen	McLaren
	2 Eddie Irvine	Ferrari
	3 David Coulthard	McLaren
	4 Damon Hill	Jordan
	5 Heinz-Harald Frentzen	Williams
	6 Jacques Villeneuve	Williams

Considering Japan's involvement with the world's automotive market from the 1960s and the participation of Honda's Formula One team, amazingly it was not until the middle of the 1970s that Japan hosted a Grand Prix. Even then, its race fans enjoyed just two races, in 1976 and 1977, before Formula One moved on again. It was not until 1987 that it

held its third Grand Prix and became established on the World Championship calendar.

That first race was held at the Fuji Speedway at the foot of the sacred Mount Fuji volcano. Mario Andretti splashed through the rain to win, but few will remember that. What they will recall is that James Hunt finished

ALMOST THERE: The sight of the Ferris Wheel marks the last chicane and the arrival of the start/finish straight

third and that this was enough to give him the world title as Niki Lauda had pulled in to the pits and refused to race on because of the conditions. Armchair enthusiasts should note that it was his title success that encouraged the BBC to upgrade its piecemeal coverage of Formula One and screen every race. A year later, Gilles Villeneuve's Ferrari somersaulted over a fence and killed two people, putting a question-mark over Fuji's suitability for Formula One racing.

When the Japanese Grand Prix re-emerged, it was held at Suzuka, where it has remained to this day, resisting the claim from the TI Circuit that it should take over the slot. In fact, the TI Circuit held a race under the guise of the Pacific Grand Prix in 1994. But Suzuka is the real stronghold of Japanese racing, with the once-crazy demand for tickets now returning.

Home of the shoot-out

Usually the last or penultimate race of the season, the Japanese Grand Prix has seen more than its share of title shoot-outs, including two between Ayrton Senna and Alain Prost in 1989 and 1990 that saw them collide on both occasions, with Prost claiming the first title as a result and Senna the second. In 1997, when it was the penultimate race, it provided drama aplenty even before it started. Jacques Villeneuve had arrived with a nine-point advantage over Michael Schumacher, so all he had to do was finish ahead of him and the title would be his.

But first he had to start the race, and he got himself disqualified from doing so by driving at unabated speed past a waved yellow flag during practice. Only when Williams appealed against this decision was he allowed to start, and the race was packed with interesting tactics as Eddie Irvine did everything in his power to ensure his Ferrari team-mate Schumacher took the maximum haul of points.

Last year, Mika Hakkinen arrived with a four-point lead over Michael Schumacher. He had his race to the title made all the easier when first Schumacher stalled and had to start from the rear of the grid, and then he retired when he had a massive blow-out, leaving Hakkinen to cruise to victory ahead of Irvine.

While many circuits look similar in plan-form, Suzuka is very different.

It's a fast and very technical circuit, requiring endless testing for a driver to learn its many intricacies. Experience counts, so those Formula One drivers who spent part of their careers racing in Japanese championships have a clear advantage, such as Irvine, Villeneuve, Heinz-Harald Frentzen, Mika Salo, Ralf Schumacher and, of course, the Japanese drivers.

A drivers' circuit

The track slopes down to the first corner, a double-apex right-hander out of which the drivers race into a series of third-gear esses – through which drivers can make up fractions of a second if they get it right. A fifth-gear left-hander is next, then on down to Degner Curve, a fast right-hander that takes the track under a bridge, through a kink into a left-hand hairpin. Then it's a curving, flat-out blast to Spoon Curve. This is a long, tight left-hander, and it's crucial to get right as it opens out on to the fastest section of the track. Half-way up the straight to the final chicane comes 130R, a sixth-gear corner taken at around 160mph. The final corner is the ultra-tight chicane at which Damon Hill dived past Heinz-Harald Frentzen on the final lap of last year's Grand Prix, before the track bends right on to the start/finish straight. The drivers love it.

HERO OF THE TRACK

Aguri Suzuki gave Japanese Formula One fans their greatest moment when he climbed on to the Suzuka podium after the 1990 Japanese GP. And, what's more, he pulled off this feat driving a Larrousse... Still, it was a better car than the one he drove for Zakspeed in 1989. Aguri went on to race for Footwork and Ligier, but never visited another podium. He is now a TV commentator and a promoter of young Japanese talent.

Mika Hakkinen versus Michael Schumacher, McLaren versus Ferrari: that was the story of the 1998 season. And almost nothing came between these warring factions in one of the most gripping title battles that Formula One has seen for many a year.

However, it didn't look as though there was a ghost of a chance of such a duel after the opening race in Melbourne, when the McLarens creamed the opposition, lapping the entire field. The championship would surely come down to a straight contest between Hakkinen and his team-mate David Coulthard, with the other 10 teams left to fight over the scraps.

Yet, on that day back in March an important thing happened: Hakkinen mistakenly thought he'd been called into the pits and made an erroneous pit stop that cost him the lead. However, Coulthard kept to a pre-race agreement that whichever of them led into the first corner would win the race, and so let Hakkinen past for victory. The difference between first place and second is four points, and these would become crucial for the Finn.

Indeed, after a Ferrari fightback that began when Schumacher muscled Coulthard out of the way to win the third race in Argentina and was then augmented by three wins in a row mid-season, the German arrived at the final round in Japan just four points behind Hakkinen. Yes, those four gifted points from Australia had come home to roost, and this put all the pressure on Schumacher, who knew that he had to win, come what may, to be champion. And, even if he did, Hakkinen was going to have to finish third or lower. So he was relying heavily on team-mate Eddie Irvine — very heavily. Then, fate would have it that the pressure of the occasion got not to the title show-down rookie Hakkinen, but to the experienced title-fighter Schumacher, as he stalled at the start and was forced to start the race from the back of the grid. The big battle was over, and not only had Hakkinen landed the World Championship title that had looked to be his right from his early days in car racing, but McLaren had returned to the top for the first time since Ayrton Senna's reign in 1991, and Mercedes for the first time since Juan Manuel Fangio was top dog in 1955.

What should be remembered is that

AUSTRALIAN GP ARGENTINIAN GP BRAZILIAN GP SAN MAI
BRITISH GP AUSTRIAN GP GERMAN GP HUNGARIAN G

REVIEW OF 1998

McLaren started the year – the first with narrower chassis and grooved tyres – with the best package, courtesy of ex-Williams designer Adrian Newey and superior Mercedes horsepower. The drivers weren't that bad either... Inevitably with new regulations, one team will steal a march. But such is the pace of progress in Formula One that the others always catch up. Well, at least those with the budgets to turn things around.

Ferrari was the team with the most in reserve, with designer Rory Byrne producing literally a new aerodynamic tweak for every race in the quest to give Schumacher and Irvine a car with which they could have a shot at the McLarens. Perhaps the greatest breakthrough, though, was the arrival of wider Goodyear

front tyres in the third race, helping Schumacher to claw back the gap to the Bridgestone-shod McLarens.

And what of the rest? Well, 1998 marked a three-way shoot-out for third place in the Constructors' Cup between Williams, Benetton and Jordan. Yes, the 1997 champions had fallen from grace, with Williams struggling now that it was using ex-works Renault engines badged as Mecachromes. Indeed, so were Benetton, and both teams suffered from a lack of grunt when it mattered against McLaren and Ferrari – and, as the year progressed, against the Mugen Honda-powered Jordans. Outgoing champion Jacques Villeneuve and Heinz-Harald Frentzen struggled all year, finishing no higher than third between them, while Giancarlo

Fisichella scored Benetton's best results with a pair of second-place finishes.

But it was relative newcomers Jordan who hit the jackpot, with their day of days coming in the crash-torn Belgian Grand Prix at Spa, when Damon Hill led Ralf Schumacher home for the team's first win. Combined with a run of strong results, this propelled the team that failed to score until the second half of the season past Benetton into fourth overall in the Constructors' Championship at the final race.

As ever, the teams beyond the top five were simply struggling for pride and hope in their wake, seeking the odd points-scoring result to guarantee themselves travel money for the following year. Survival rather than glory is the watchword for the second half of the grid.

GP SPANISH GP MONACO GP CANADIAN GP FRENCH GP
BELGIAN GP ITALIAN GP LUXEMBOURG GP JAPANESE GP

F1

THE YEAR IN PICTURES

AUSTRALIAN GP

THE MCLAREN SHUFFLE

RACE RESULTS

ROUND 1 AT ALBERT PARK,
MELBOURNE, MARCH 8, 1998

(AFTER 58 LAPS)

Pos	Driver	Team
1	MIKA HAKKINEN	McLaren
2	DAVID COULTHARD	McLaren
3	HEINZ-HARALD FRENTZEN	Williams
4	EDDIE IRVINE	Ferrari
5	JACQUES VILLENEUVE	Williams
6	JOHNNY HERBERT	Sauber

FASTEST LAP: Hakkinen, 1m 31.649s
(128.84mph/207.34km/h)
WEATHER CONDITIONS: Hot and sunny

McLaren dominated in Australia in such a way that no one else had a look-in. But they angered many by instructing David Coulthard to slow down to let Mika Hakkinen win.

Those who noticed how McLaren had dragged itself on to the pace at the end of the 1997 season were convinced that the team would fare even better when it had its first Adrian Newey-penned chassis. And they were right, for Hakkinen and Coulthard were the class of the field every time the cars went on to Melbourne's Albert Park circuit.

Sitting pretty on the front row ahead of Michael Schumacher's Ferrari and the Williams of reigning World Champion Jacques Villeneuve, the drivers were confident enough to have entered into a pact that whichever of them entered the first corner in front would be allowed to stay there, barring disasters. A strange agreement, perhaps, but one that would prevent them from risking racing each other.

And so, with Hakkinen getting away well from pole position, it looked to be his race as Coulthard tucked in behind, with the chasing pack growing smaller in their mirrors at an astonishing rate. This gap was soon enlarged further when Schumacher pulled up, his engine smoking. But Villeneuve was no better equipped to keep the McLarens in sight, and continued to drop away. Indeed, after the first round of pit stops, he found himself behind team-mate Heinz-Harald Frentzen, Eddie Irvine's Ferrari and Giancarlo Fisichella's Benetton. And then he was lapped...

Still the McLaren steamroller crushed the opposition – until lap 36, when Hakkinen came into the pits, but drove straight through without stopping. He had misheard a call over the radio

and was now second. But there was that pre-race agreement to honour and, amazingly, Coulthard remained a man of his word – even though their reversal of positions was the team's fault, not his own. He slowed enough for Hakkinen to hit the front with three laps to go, angering those who had placed bets on the race and sending volatile race organizer Ron Walker into orbit.

Frentzen was third, a lap down, showing how McLaren had set a new target for the others to aim at. Many reckoned they had never seen dominance like it, and were talking of a McLaren whitewash even more impressive than its 15 wins from 16 starts in 1988. For the record, Irvine finished fourth – right on Frentzen's tail – with Villeneuve a disillusioned fifth and Johnny Herbert scoring the final point for Sauber.

MIKA'S WINNING START: It looked as though Hakkinen had blown it, but team-mate Coulthard let him through to win

BRAZILIAN GP

MIKA ALL THE WAY

RACE RESULTS
ROUND 2 AT INTERLAGOS, SAO PAULO, MARCH 29, 1998

(AFTER 72 LAPS)

Pos	Driver	Team
1	MIKA HAKKINEN	McLaren
2	DAVID COULTHARD	McLaren
3	MICHAEL SCHUMACHER	Ferrari
4	ALEXANDER WURZ	Benetton
5	HEINZ-HARALD FRENTZEN	Williams
6	GIANCARLO FISICHELLA	Benetton

FASTEST LAP: Hakkinen, 1m 19.337s (120.70mph/194.24km/h)
WEATHER CONDITIONS: Hot and sunny

Mika Hakkinen's wins at Jerez in 1997 and then in Melbourne in the new season were seen as coming his way with the assistance of others. But, not so this one in Brazil.

There was still a stink in the air when the teams arrived in Sao Paulo for the Brazilian Grand Prix, following the place-swapping between Coulthard and Hakkinen in Australia. However, the sport's governing body had clarified the rules in the interim so that a team's drivers could swap position in a race only if it wasn't going to influence the outcome of the title race.

But there was another furore surrounding McLaren, as Ferrari had protested about its braking system – which enabled the drivers to apply the brakes on the rear wheels independently, and thus assist both turn-in to corners and traction out of them. As a result, the team agreed not to use the system at any stage over the weekend. However, team boss Ron Dennis was livid that the system had been approved on four occasions by the FIA technical delegate, Charlie Whiting, and was now being declared illegal by the three stewards in office for the Brazilian Grand Prix.

However, on to less political on-track matters. McLaren thumbed its nose at its challengers by placing both cars on the front row, with polesitter Hakkinen over a second up on the third-placed Williams of Heinz-Harald Frentzen. Michael Schumacher edged out Benetton's Alexander Wurz to claim fourth on the grid.

The race proved to be simplicity itself for Hakkinen and Coulthard, who ran first and second throughout, not falling back behind third-placed Wurz even when they made their one pit-stop apiece. Yet, although they finished just a second apart, Coulthard never looked capable of passing Hakkinen for the lead, the Finn holding the upper hand all weekend.

Wurz proved to be one of the pleasant diversions in an otherwise processional event, impressing everyone with a fabulous dive past Frentzen into the first corner after his one stop. However, he was made to settle for fourth place as Schumacher atoned for a poor start, which saw him sixth into the first corner, to take third position after his second stop. For the record, though, he was exactly a minute adrift of the McLarens. Team-mate Eddie Irvine also adopted a two-stop strategy, but this didn't work for him as he became caught in traffic after his second stop; he finished eighth behind Frentzen, Giancarlo Fisichella and Jacques Villeneuve, all of whom had been lapped.

MCLARENS OUT IN FRONT: Hakkinen leads team-mate Coulthard and Williams' Frentzen at the start

ARGENTINIAN GP

REVIEW OF THE
1998 SEASON

106

ARGY BARGY

RACE RESULTS

**ROUND 3 AT BUENOS AIRES,
APRIL 12, 1998**

(AFTER 72 LAPS)

Pos	Driver	Team
1	MICHAEL SCHUMACHER	Ferrari
2	MIKA HAKKINEN	McLaren
3	EDDIE IRVINE	Ferrari
4	ALEXANDER WURZ	Benetton
5	JEAN ALESI	Sauber
6	DAVID COULTHARD	McLaren

FASTEST LAP: Wurz, 1m 28.178s
(108.03mph/173.84km/h)
WEATHER CONDITIONS: Cloudy and
warm

Ferrari team leader Michael Schumacher showed that he meant business when he barged David Coulthard out of the lead, and motored on to dent McLaren's supremacy.

Nothing upsets the people in charge of Formula One more than domination by one team: it's terrible for those all-important television viewing figures. So, it's not surprising that these people view Michael Schumacher as their saviour – the man who can drag a lesser car into contention and keep the racing exciting, as he did right up to the final round in 1997, when his Ferrari was the thorn in the side of Williams's Jacques Villeneuve. And at Jerez, Schumacher showed at that he's not scared of using robust tactics to stay in the hunt.

'Schuey' was at it again in Buenos Aires, gaining victory from an event that most people thought would be another formality for McLaren. Could McLaren achieve the unthinkable and win every race in the calender? The fact that Schumacher used bodily contact

to force his way into the lead made those at the top happier still. After all, they consider any publicity to be good publicity.

Whereas Hakkinen had been McLaren's top performer in Brazil, it was Coulthard's turn to be the team's number one in Argentina, on a circuit on which he always shines. Indeed, fans were surprised when Schumacher put his Ferrari on the grid alongside pole position Coulthard, with Hakkinen third.

However, Hakkinen made amends by moving past a slow-starting Schumacher into second. Meanwhile, Coulthard started to eke out an advantage, but Schumacher made it through to second place on the second lap and set off after the Scot. At the start of the fifth lap, he was right with him and, noticing that Coulthard had run wide at the first corner on the previous lap, decided there was a possibility he

may do so again and dived for the inside into the hairpin. He slammed into the side of Coulthard, spinning him down to sixth, while Schumacher himself motored on unaffected. It was, as ITV commentator Martin Brundle said, "a pretty rude manoeuvre".

The race then became one between a twice-stopping Schumacher and Hakkinen, who was on a one-stop strategy. And Schumacher's plan proved to be the correct one, as he emerged in front following his second stop, after Hakkinen lost time behind Heinz-Harald Frentzen, and stayed there to win.

Coulthard was slowed by gearbox problems and lost further ground when he tangled with Jacques Villeneuve, putting the Canadian out, while the Scot collected the solitary point for sixth place behind Eddie Irvine, Alexander Wurz and Sauber's Jean Alesi.

POINT OF CONTACT: David Coulthard discovers just how badly Michael Schumacher wanted to take the lead

SAN MARINO GP

KEEPING HIS COOL

Soaring oil temperatures on David Coulthard's McLaren forced the Scot to drive a canny race at Imola, but he hung on to thwart Ferrari's charging Michael Schumacher.

RACE RESULTS
ROUND 4 AT IMOLA, APRIL 26, 1998
(AFTER 62 LAPS)

Pos	Driver	Team
1	DAVID COULTHARD	McLaren
2	MICHAEL SCHUMACHER	Ferrari
3	EDDIE IRVINE	Ferrari
4	JACQUES VILLENEUVE	Williams
5	HEINZ-HARALD FRENTZEN	Williams
6	JEAN ALESI	Sauber

FASTEST LAP: M. Schumacher
1m29.345s (123.44mph/198.65km/h)
WEATHER CONDITIONS: Warm and sunny

McLaren's dominance in the first two Grands Prix of the season must have been giving the organizers of the San Marino Grand Prix a few sleepless nights: they would never fill Imola if Ferrari didn't have a chance of success. So they were thanking their lucky stars when Michael Schumacher won in Argentina, and were praying that he'd match the feat on home ground. History will record that the German failed in this quest, but not by much.

It was back to business for McLaren in qualifying, with Coulthard outpacing Hakkinen for pole, and Ferrari's Schumacher and Eddie Irvine keeping things neat by qualifying third and fourth. However, the men in red had hoped for better, and had followed Tyrrell's lead in fitting 'side-wings' – x-shaped wings bolted atop the sidepods. But these appendages didn't produce enough of a gain to topple the McLarens and, with Jordan and Sauber also sprouting these peculiar side-wings, the sport's governing body voted to ban them the day after the race, as they felt that they would be unsafe if a driver suffered a side-on impact. Also, it was said, they considered them to be ugly, and they were quite right on that count.

The race was simplicity itself for Coulthard as he controlled proceedings ahead of Mika Hakkinen, with Schumacher split from Irvine by Jacques Villeneuve's Williams. But on lap 17 Hakkinen retired to the pits, and the garage door was immediately rolled down to conceal his problem. It later proved to have been gearbox failure.

Unaware of his team-mate's problem, Coulthard motored on ahead of Schumacher until the German emerged from his second stop and started to fly, eating into the Scot's 20-second advantage at a rate of a second per lap. Debris in a sidepod had sent Coulthard's oil

SCOTLAND THE BRAVE: David Coulthard controlled the race, but had to watch his temperature lights carefully

cooler temperature soaring, and team boss Ron Dennis kept sprinting from the pit wall to the McLaren garage to check on the telemetry, so that Coulthard could be instructed how much he could afford to ease off to save his engine. Yet, every so often, Coulthard would match Schumacher's pace, just to show who was boss, and duly recorded the win he had clearly been due in the season's first few races.

Irvine sent the Ferrari fans home happy by taking the final place on the podium, with the Williams duo of Villeneuve and Frentzen the only other unlapped runners.

SPANISH GP

RACE RESULTS

ROUND 5 AT CATALUNYA,
BARCELONA, MAY 5, 1998

(AFTER 65 LAPS)

Pos	Driver	Team
1	MIKA HAKKINEN	McLaren
2	DAVID COULTHARD	McLaren
3	MICHAEL SCHUMACHER	Ferrari
4	ALEXANDER WURZ	Benetton
5	RUBENS BARRICHELLO	Stewart
6	JACQUES VILLENEUVE	Williams

FASTEST LAP: Hakkinen, 1m 24.275s
(125.50mph/201.97km/h)
WEATHER CONDITIONS: Hot and sunny

HAKKINEN AT EASE

Mika Hakkinen and David Coulthard duly reeled off another McLaren one-two in Spain, as a distant Michael Schumacher proved to be the best of the rest for Ferrari.

Hakkinen showed that the best way of recovering from retiring from one race is to dominate the next. And this is what he did in the Spanish Grand Prix, proving fastest every time his McLaren ventured out on to the Circuit de Catalunya. Indeed, he outqualified team-mate David Coulthard by 0.7 seconds, with Schumacher a further 0.8 seconds back. The race proved simplicity itself as Hakkinen helped himself to maximum points, and Coulthard followed him home 10 seconds behind to give McLaren the full haul of 16 points towards its bid for the constructors' title.

Indeed, such was McLaren's control of proceedings that spectators had to look elsewhere for their excitement. Schumacher tried to provide some by making a wretched start and falling back from third on the grid to fifth behind Eddie Irvine (up from sixth after one of his regular rocket getaways) and Benetton's Giancarlo Fisichella. And this was how they ran until their first pit stops, when Irvine delayed Fisichella sufficiently for his team-mate Schumacher to emerge ahead, in third position.

Fisichella wasn't impressed by this act and set about Irvine. But his attempted passing manoeuvre around the outside failed when neither saw fit to back off, and they speared off into the gravel trap where they entered into a heated debate. And so Fisichella's team-mate, Alexander Wurz, inherited fourth place, which he held all the way to the chequered flag.

Rubens Barrichello may have been disappointed that his Stewart had been lapped, but he was delighted with his drive nonetheless, bringing his car him home in fifth place ahead of the Williams of reigning World Champion Jacques Villeneuve. While this emphasized that the Stewart team was making progress after a poor start to the season, it suggested that Williams was actually becoming less competitive by the race, struggling to get its chassis to behave. Add to that the fact that the Bridgestone tyres used by McLaren and Benetton in particular seemed to have the edge, especially in hot conditions, and you can imagine the despair setting in at Williams.

Team morale was not what it had been when they were sweeping all before them in the early 1990s, and Heinz-Harald Frentzen was coming under increasing pressure after finishing eighth, two laps behind Hakkinen. He had qualified 13th and Villeneuve 10th, but the Canadian got stuck in during the race while Frentzen appeared out of sorts after colliding with Jean Alesi on the first lap, and was forced to make an extra pit stop.

RAIN IN SPAIN: Hakkinen, Coulthard and Schumacher spray the bubbly on the podium after the McLaren men dominated proceedings again

MONACO GP

MORE OF THE SAME

Mika Hakkinen had never finished a Monaco Grand Prix before. But this time he got everything right, winning easily once his McLaren team-mate David Coulthard had retired.

RACE RESULTS

ROUND 6 AT MONACO, MAY 24, 1998

(AFTER 78 LAPS)

Pos	Driver	Team
1	MIKA HAKKINEN	McLaren
2	GIANCARLO FISICHELLA	Benetton
3	EDDIE IRVINE	Ferrari
4	MIKA SALO	Arrows
5	JACQUES VILLENEUVE	Williams
6	PEDRO DINIZ	Arrows

FASTEST LAP: Hakkinen, 1m 22.948s (90.79mph/146.11km/h)
WEATHER CONDITIONS: Hot and sunny

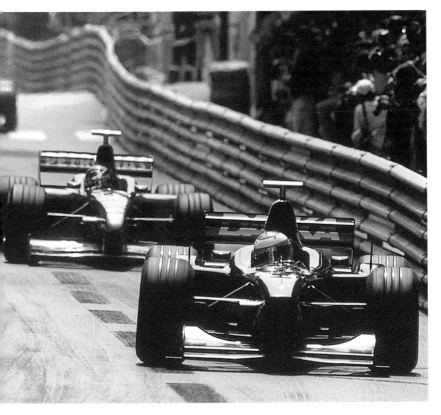

FLYING ARROWS: Mika Salo showed his skills again at Monaco, finishing fourth after a one-stop run

It's amazing how fast people forget what has gone before. After all, when Mika Hakkinen went out on to the track at Monaco in May 1998 he was expected to win. Yet this was a driver who had failed to finish the Monaco Grand Prix on any of his previous six attempts, and had never won a Grand Prix at all until he was gifted the final race of 1997 at Jerez. Still, times change fast in Formula One, and few fancied Monaco-meister Michael Schumacher's chances.

One day into the event, Schumacher's chances had receded further, for he crashed in Casino Square in the untimed sessions on the Thursday, and had a driveshaft break on his first lap in Saturday's untimed sessions. Having lost this valuable track time, he did well to qualify fourth behind Hakkinen, David Coulthard and Benetton's delighted Giancarlo Fisichella, with Eddie Irvine slumping to seventh after a shunt.

The race was a formality for the Finn, as he led throughout. His afternoon would have been far tougher had Coulthard not disappeared from his tail on lap 18 when his engine blew.

This elevated Fisichella to second, while Schumacher fought with Alexander Wurz for fourth place. The two-time World Champion bounced his Ferrari off Wurz's Benetton at the Loews hairpin, but the Austrian fought back and dived in front again at the next corner, only to slide wide and let Schumacher move back inside as they rounded Portier. Perhaps as a result of this impact, Wurz had his suspension break in the tunnel five laps later, leaving him a passenger as his car thumped into the barriers.

The incident also put paid to Schumacher's race, as it damaged his rear suspension and he retired to the pits. But, as he tried to climb out of the car, he was pushed back in by team chief Ross Brawn. Lengthy repairs ensued and he emerged for what would effectively be a test session. On the last lap, he even tested the strength of his Ferrari's nose by hitting Pedro Diniz, and was finally classified 10th. Fisichella claimed second and was lucky to do so, as he spun at Rascasse with 17 laps to go. Fortunately, he spun the car around to face the right direction, and got going again before Irvine could get by.

Perhaps the most amazing result was Mika Salo's fourth place for Arrows, one position better than he'd managed for Tyrrell in 1997. In spite of his assault by Schumacher, Salo's team-mate Diniz was sixth, just a handful of seconds behind Villeneuve who had started 13th. Heinz-Harald Frentzen, on the other hand, started fourth but crashed out of the race.

CANADIAN GP

THE START OF A RUN

RACE RESULTS

ROUND 7 AT CIRCUIT GILLES
VILLENEUVE, JUNE 7, 1998

(AFTER 69 LAPS)

Pos	Driver	Team
1	MICHAEL SCHUMACHER	Ferrari
2	GIANCARLO FISICHELLA	Benetton
3	EDDIE IRVINE	Ferrari
4	ALEXANDER WURZ	Benetton
5	RUBENS BARRICHELLO	Stewart
6	JAN MAGNUSSEN	Stewart

FASTEST LAP: M. Schumacher, 1m 19.379s
(124.58mph/200.49km/h)

WEATHER CONDITIONS: Cool, overcast
and windy

The Canadian Grand Prix will be remembered for a spectacular crash at the first corner, and also for the start of a three-race winning streak for Ferrari's Michael Schumacher.

Third on the grid, Michael Schumacher might have reckoned that he could keep the McLarens of pole-sitter David Coulthard and Mika Hakkinen in his sights, but that would be all. How wrong he was, for it was at the Circuit Gilles Villeneuve that McLaren chose to stumble.

Both Coulthard and Hakkinen made good starts, but they had to do it all again as the race was stopped after a huge first-corner accident. Ralf Schumacher, starting fifth in his Jordan, had stalled, and those behind him were bunched as they avoided his car. Then Heinz-Harald Frentzen jinked to the inside as Jacques Villeneuve locked up. This caused Jean Alesi to move left too, and this left an over-ambitious Alexander Wurz with little space to go, getting on to the grass before hitting Alesi's Sauber and rolling across the front of the pack. Jarno Trulli's Prost and Johnny Herbert's Sauber were also involved.

The race got underway again, but Ralf Schumacher spun into the first corner, and sent those behind rattling over the kerbs in avoidance. Alesi and Trulli were again involved, this time with the Italian's Prost coming to rest atop the Frenchman's Sauber.

Ahead of this fracas, Schumacher had got the jump on Hakkinen to grab second, but the Finn was in trouble and pulled into the pits at the end of the lap, his gearbox having failed as he left the grid.

Eddie Irvine had picked up a puncture and lost ground – pitting at the end of the first lap – but not as much as he could have done, as the safety car had been deployed. Once the safety car had pulled off, Coulthard edged clear of Schumacher, and this bode well as he was planning to stop just once compared with Schumacher's two-stop plan. But this became academic when the Scot pulled off on lap 18 after his throttle linkage broke.

Thus Schumacher took the lead – for one lap, at any rate, before he made the first of his stops, handing the lead to Giancarlo Fisichella. However, when he rejoined the track he swerved across to the far side and put Frentzen off on to the grass in the braking zone for the first corner, and the Williams driver beached his car in the gravel trap. Schumacher was awarded a stop-go penalty, and amazingly emerged from the pit lane in third place behind Fisichella and Damon Hill's Jordan. Schumacher then fought a fierce battle before moving past Hill and setting off after Fisichella. When Fisichella made his one and only pit stop, Schumacher took a lead he was not to lose…

Irvine completed Ferrari's day by working his way up to third, and both Stewarts collected points. Local hero Villeneuve led the race for a short distance when he passed Fisichella, but a couple of incidents dropped him to his eventual 10th place.

OVER AND OUT: Alexander Wurz went barrell-rolling at the first start. He managed a fourth place in the spare Benetton

FRENCH GP

FAIR AND SQUARE

Michael Schumacher grabbed the lead at the second start and team-mate Eddie Irvine helped him escape to victory.

RACE RESULTS
ROUND 8 AT MAGNY-COURS,
JUNE 28, 1998

(AFTER 71 LAPS)

Pos	Driver	Team
1	MICHAEL SCHUMACHER	Ferrari
2	EDDIE IRVINE	Ferrari
3	MIKA HAKKINEN	McLaren
4	JACQUES VILLENEUVE	Williams
5	ALEXANDER WURZ	Benetton
6	DAVID COULTHARD	McLaren

FASTEST LAP: Coulthard, 1m 17.523s
(122.64mph/197.36km/h)
WEATHER CONDITIONS: Warm and sunny

If his win in Canada was due to the failure of the McLarens, Michael Schumacher was helped only at the start in France.

The Ferrari fightback against McLaren looked ever more convincing at Magny-Cours. As ever, revised parts were being tried on the car, with a new front-wing endplate being introduced, along with tidied-up rear bodywork and a new rear diffuser. And they clearly worked, Schumacher managing to outqualify David Coulthard to line up second on the grid behind Mika Hakkinen, with team-mate Eddie Irvine a competitive fourth.

However, after failing to outrun Hakkinen on the dash to the first corner, Schumacher was offered another chance when the race was stopped. Gallingly for McLaren, this was because of a breakdown in the starting procedure triggered by Jos Verstappen, who was back in Formula One as a replacement for the supposedly out-of-form Jan Magnussen at Stewart, and had stalled on the grid. In an attempt to illuminate the yellow abort lights, the starter switched off the red lights and that set the field on its way.

Ironically, by the time the pack came swarming on to the start/finish straight at the end of the lap, the Dutchman's car had been pushed to the side of the track and was no danger to anyone.

However, the race was still stopped and Hakkinen's day took a turn for the worse on the restart, when not only was he beaten into the first corner by Schumacher but by Irvine as well.

Irvine is probably the most faithful number two driver in Formula One – although he is handsomely rewarded for this role – and he duly delayed the McLarens as Schumacher

FERRARI IN STEREO: Michael Schumacher was delighted to win and was doubly pleased that Eddie Irvine kept the McLarens at bay

raced away in the lead, regularly pulling out a second for every lap that went by. Lap after lap, Hakkinen champed at the bit in his wake until he slipped into second on lap 19 after Irvine was held up – only to try just that little bit too hard into the final corner and spin, letting Irvine and Coulthard through. Although Hakkinen soon passed his team-mate for third as they made their first pit stops, he climbed no higher despite numerous attempts to

relegate Irvine from second place.

And this was how they finished – with the exception of Coulthard, who hit refuelling problems on his second stop, and was required to pit twice more. This left him with just one point for sixth behind Jacques Villeneuve and Alexander Wurz after the Scot overtook Jean Alesi on the final lap. This was Ferrari's first one-two since Alain Prost and Nigel Mansell filled the top two spots for the team at Jerez in 1990.

BRITISH GP

TOTAL CONFUSION

RACE RESULTS

ROUND 9 AT SILVERSTONE,
JULY 12, 1998

(AFTER 60 LAPS)

Pos	Driver	Team
1	MICHAEL SCHUMACHER	Ferrari
2	MIKA HAKKINEN	McLaren
3	EDDIE IRVINE	Ferrari
4	ALEXANDER WURZ	Benetton
5	GIANCARLO FISICHELLA	Benetton
6	RALF SCHUMACHER	Jordan

FASTEST LAP: M. Schumacher, 1m 35.704s (120.15mph/193.35km/h)

WEATHER CONDITIONS: Cool, wet and windy

Michael Schumacher and Ferrari again overcame a penalty to win a Grand Prix, this time controversially taking their penalty *after* the finish line at a soaking Silverstone.

Michael Schumacher made it three wins in a row at the British Grand Prix. While his performance in dreadful conditions was awe-inspiring – as he lapped fastest when the track was at its wettest – the race belonged to Mika Hakkinen, and it was seen by many as a travesty of justice that the McLaren man wasn't adjudged the winner.

Hakkinen qualified on pole, but David Coulthard could manage only fourth, slower than Schumacher and Jacques Villeneuve. Hakkinen led away at the start, with Coulthard and a fast-starting Jean Alesi relegating Villeneuve. Four laps later, Coulthard moved past Schumacher at Abbey, then the Ferraris dropped away, both struggling on 'full dry' set-ups in the damp – albeit with Eddie Irvine climbing from tenth to sixth after a troubled start from fifth on the grid.

Light rain started to fall after a dozen laps and this became heavy, sending cars scurrying into the pits. However, alone among the front-runners, Hakkinen opted for full wet tyres while the others stuck with intermediates, Irvine climbing to fourth after this flurry of pitting activity. Coulthard then caught Hakkinen, but conditions deteriorated and Hakkinen pulled clear. Coulthard promptly spun.

Every team opted for full wets at their second stops, except for Williams, which stuck with intermediates. Two laps later, Villeneuve was in again, this time for full wets, dropping out of the points in the process. Hakkinen then had a grassy moment at Bridge as conditions worsened. He rejoined, but others were not so lucky. Five laps later, the safety car came out. In an instant, Hakkinen lost his 40-second advantage. To make matters worse, his car had been damaged and he was fearful of whether he would be able to hold

HOLDING POSITIONS: Mika Hakkinen heads the field behind the safety car after extremely wet conditions brought it out and cost him a 40-second lead

off Schumacher when they were released.

And when they were, it proved that he couldn't, Hakkinen running off at Becketts to let Schumacher take a lead he didn't look like losing. But Schumacher had been awarded a stop-go penalty for passing Alexander Wurz under the yellow flags just before the safety car had been deployed. However, the officials took ages to notify the team of this violation, and as Ferrari weren't sure if a ten-second penalty should just be added to his race time; they told

him to continue on his way, bringing him in for the penalty at the end of the final lap, meaning that he stopped for the prescribed ten seconds after he'd crossed the finish line. No wonder no one appeared to know who had won. Amazingly, Schumacher was declared the winner, although few understood how or why.

Completing a good day for the Schumachers, Ralf gave Jordan its first point of the season, all the more surprising as he had started at the back of the grid.

AUSTRIAN GP

BACK ON TRACK

RACE RESULTS
ROUND 10 AT A1-RING,
JULY 26, 1998

(AFTER 71 LAPS)

Pos	Driver	Team
1	MIKA HAKKINEN	McLaren
2	DAVID COULTHARD	McLaren
3	MICHAEL SCHUMACHER	Ferrari
4	EDDIE IRVINE	Ferrari
5	RALF SCHUMACHER	Jordan
6	JACQUES VILLENEUVE	Williams

FASTEST LAP: Coulthard, 1m 12.878s
(132.58mph/213.33km/h)
WEATHER CONDITIONS: Hot and sunny

McLaren moved back in full control for the first time since dominating the Spanish Grand Prix in May, as Hakkinen and Coulthard raced to another one-two.

That may sound as though McLaren had simply recovered from the twists of fate from which it had suffered in the three previous Grands Prix, but it was not as simple as that.

Well, not in qualifying at least, as Hakkinen slipped to third and Coulthard all the way back to 14th... Sweltering temperatures had given way to rain. The A1-Ring then started to dry out as the session advanced. Damon Hill was the first out on the track and was slipping all over the place, hitting streams of water across the undulating circuit. The rest of the drivers sat in their garages, watching and waiting. Then, with a dry line appearing in the closing minutes, they went for it, with Jean Alesi poised for Sauber's first-ever pole position until the very last car took the flag. And this, Giancarlo Fisichella's Benetton, demoted Alesi to second. Of the rest, Michael Schumacher lined up fourth, but Rubens Barrichello surprisingly placed his Stewart fifth and Mika Salo was sixth for Arrows.

Come the race, though, the weather was dry. Hakkinen made a great start and was in the lead by the time he entered the uphill first corner. Michael Schumacher had also got past Fisichella and Alesi to give chase. There was trouble behind, though, with Tyrrell's Toranosuke Takagi scattering the tail end of the field. Up to the second corner, and Pedro Diniz hit Coulthard, both of them spinning. Worse was to follow, as he also clipped his Arrows team-mate Mika Salo, who spun his car around to rejoin and took the end off Coulthard's nose, necessitating a pit-stop for the Scot. He was fortunate that the safety car came out while the debris was being cleared.

When the field was set on its way again, Schumacher fought hard to pass Hakkinen, for he was on a two-stop strategy and reckoned the

Finn would be stopping only once. Then he pushed too hard and ran wide through the penultimate corner, damaging the nose of his car when he landed. A subsequent pit-stop dropped him to the tail of the field and let Fisichella back to second ahead of Irvine and, amazingly, Coulthard...

Fisichella was not long for the race, though, clashing with Alesi at the second corner as he brought his Benetton back out after a pit stop. Both were out of the race on the spot. Then, when Irvine pitted, Coulthard moved into a second place that he would keep right to the finish. If that was impressive, so was Schumacher's fightback to third, something that he achieved with three laps to go when he moved ahead of his team-mate, who conveniently developed brake problems.

FIRST LAP FRACAS: Mika Salo takes off David Coulthard's front wing on the opening lap before the Scot pitted and stormed through to second

GERMAN GP

MCLAREN MUSCLE

RACE RESULTS

AT HOCKENHEIM,
AUGUST 2, 1998

(AFTER 45 LAPS)

Pos	Driver	Team
1	MIKA HAKKINEN	McLaren
2	DAVID COULTHARD	McLaren
3	JACQUES VILLENEUVE	Williams
4	DAMON HILL	Jordan
5	MICHAEL SCHUMACHER	Ferrari
6	RALF SCHUMACHER	Jordan

FASTEST LAP: Coulthard, 1m 46.116s
(143.84mph/231.44km/h)

WEATHER CONDITIONS: Hot and sunny

McLaren's fifth one-two of the season pushed Mika Hakkinen into a dominant position, especially as Michael Schumacher endured a thoroughly torrid time on home ground.

The very place at which Michael Schumacher wished to shine was, obviously, in front of his fervently patriotic German fans. The German Grand Prix was therefore extremely important to the Ferrari driver, especially as his popularity at home had waned since his clash with Jacques Villeneuve in the 1997 finale at Jerez. So the German Grand Prix must have been an unmitigated disaster for him.

The McLarens were always going to be strong here, with Adrian Newey's extremely aerodynamically efficient chassis expected to prove the class of the field down the circuit's endless straights when combined with Mercedes's ample horsepower. And so it proved, with Hakkinen taking pole position ahead of Coulthard. However, the red car in third on the grid was not Schumacher's Ferrari but Jacques Villeneuve's Williams, now more

competitive in long-wheelbase format. And the Schumacher occupying fourth place was not Michael but Ralf, the younger of the brothers coming out of Michael's shadow.

In fact, Michael Schumacher started ninth after a series of disasters. Firstly, he tried Ferrari's new long-wheelbase chassis on the Friday. Rejecting this car, he started afresh in the untimed sessions on the Saturday, only to spin off on his first lap. Then he had engine failure early in the second session, taking away valuable track time. There were also various mutterings that the Ferraris (with Irvine sixth) were off the pace as McLaren had threatened to protest about the Italian team's new braking system, and some were sure that it had been removed to the team's obvious detriment.

Come the race, the McLarens were dominant, running first and second throughout – and only

took single pit-stops. Ralf Schumacher looked to be the only driver capable of troubling them in the first part of the race, but although he could stay with them he couldn't pass them. It came as no surprise that he had gambled on a two-stop strategy, and was running with a light fuel load. Villeneuve took over in third place when the Jordan made the first of these stops, and this was where he stayed to the finish, even catching the McLarens until his differential started playing up. And the reason he was able to catch the McLarens was that Hakkinen's car hadn't taken on enough fuel at its stop, and the Finn had to back off to ease his fuel consumption, with Coulthard dutifully doing likewise.

Proving that one stop was better than two, Damon Hill came through to take his first points of the year, finishing fourth in front of the two Schumachers, with Michael ahead of Ralf.

PODIUM PARTY TIME: Jacques Villeneuve joins McLaren's Coulthard and Hakkinen on the podium after the race

HUNGARIAN GP

FERRARI'S WINNING TACTICS

RACE RESULTS

ROUND 12 AT HUNGARORING,
AUGUST 16, 1998

(AFTER 77 LAPS)

Pos	Driver	Team
1	MICHAEL SCHUMACHER	Ferrari
2	DAVID COULTHARD	McLaren
3	JACQUES VILLENEUVE	Williams
4	DAMON HILL	Jordan
5	HEINZ-HARALD FRENTZEN	Williams
6	MIKA HAKKINEN	McLaren

FASTEST LAP: M. Schumacher, 1m
19.286s (112.07mph/180.35km/h)
WEATHER CONDITIONS: Hot, dry and
bright

There seemed to be no way that Schumacher's Ferrari would beat the McLarens in Hungary. However, team tactician Ross Brawn forced him to make three stops, and it worked.

If Michael Schumacher was disappointed after his uncompetitive showing in the German Grand Prix, he rated his chances of success in Hungary more highly, as the Hungaroring's twisty layout lacked the high-speed corners in which the rival McLaren cars were so dominant.

The German pulled out a mighty qualifying performance to be right with Mika Hakkinen and David Coulthard, the rest of the field being almost a full second behind. But at the race-morning warm-up the McLarens lapped considerably faster than he could manage on full tanks. So the writing was on the wall, especially after the silver cars put their Mercedes horsepower down perfectly to reach the first corner in grid order, with Schumacher having missed his best chance to pass them. Still, at least he was protected from any attack from the rear as team-mate Eddie Irvine had outsprinted Damon Hill's Jordan to fill fourth place. However, Irvine didn't last long before his Ferrari's gearbox packed up. The first three then edged away, but there seemed to be nothing that Schumacher could do, with overtaking opportunities being so limited.

The first round of pit-stops came and went with no change of order, although Schumacher briefly fell back to fourth behind Jacques Villeneuve's Williams. But the German was called in early for his second stop and Coulthard was brought in to counter this move, only to emerge behind and unable to keep up with his rival. The reason for this later became clear when Schumacher came in again for a third stop: yes, he was running with a light fuel load. And it worked, for he was in front of Hakkinen, too, when the Finn emerged from his second stop.

UNBRIDLED DELIGHT: Michael Schumacher had every reason to be delighted after scoring a magnificent and unexpected tactical victory for Ferrari

It soon became clear that Hakkinen was in trouble, with something amiss with his suspension, because not only was Schumacher escaping but Mika was delaying Coulthard. After a few laps, he let the Scot past but Schumacher was long gone, and with a clear track he was able to build up the gap he required so that he would still be in front after his third stop. This he managed, with Coulthard unable to peg him back.

Third place did not got to Hakkinen, though, as he slowed even further and slipped all the way back to sixth as Villeneuve, Hill and a very ill Heinz-Harald Frentzen all came through. They all had a scare, though, when a bunch of spectators mindlessly invaded the track (causing Tagaki to spin) as they attempted to complete their final lap.

BELGIAN GP

JORDAN HITS THE BIG TIME

Damon Hill raced through the rain to give Jordan its first-ever Grand Prix win. But the 1998 Belgian GP will be remembered for an entirely different reason and a major pile-up.

RACE RESULTS
ROUND 13 AT
SPA-FRANCORCHAMPS,
AUGUST 30, 1998

(AFTER 44 LAPS)

Pos	Driver	Team
1	DAMON HILL	Jordan
2	RALF SCHUMACHER	Jordan
3	JEAN ALESI	Sauber
4	HEINZ-HARALD FRENTZEN	Williams
5	PEDRO DINIZ	Arrows
6	JARNO TRULLI	Prost

FASTEST LAP: M. Schumacher, 2m 03.766s (125.945mph/202.679km/h)
WEATHER CONDITIONS: Cold and wet, with rain becoming heavier

In the seconds that followed the field turning right through the La Source hairpin for the first time, Formula One endured one of the most violent moments in its 49-year history. David Coulthard's McLaren suddenly speared to the right, hit the wall of the old pits and came back across the track. With the cars already racing into a wall of spray, there was no chance of the pack missing him. Impact followed impact, each seemingly more sickening than the last –

and yet, with wheels still bouncing down the hill towards Eau Rouge, all the drivers managed to clamber out of their wrecked cars. A quick check revealed that 13 of the 22 starters had been involved but, amazingly, not one of them suffered anything worse than bruising. However, a lack of spare cars in some teams meant that Olivier Panis, Mika Salo, Rubens Barrichello and Ricardo Rosset did not make the restart.

Fifty minutes later, when the scene of the

carnage had been restored to normality, they tried again. This time Damon Hill rocketed past the McLarens of Mika Hakkinen and David Coulthard that occupied the front row, pushing his Jordan into the lead. An over-tentative Hakkinen went little further, being squeezed into a spin by Michael Schumacher's Ferrari as they exited La Source. He was collected by Johnny Herbert's Sauber, putting both of them out of the race straight away. McLaren's day became even worse 30 seconds later when Coulthard tangled with Alex Wurz's Benetton and he rejoined in last place, luckily catching the back of the pack when the safety car was deployed.

Ferrari filled second and third places, but Schumacher used his wet-weather expertise to catch and pass Damon Hill. Once in front, he pulled clear, but it wasn't to last, and he made a mistake when he came up to lap Coulthard – slamming into him as the Scot slowed to let him past. Both cars limped back to the pits, where an enraged Schumacher rushed along to the McLaren garage and had to be restrained as he reportedly threatened to do terrible things to the Scot.

This incident left the Jordans of Damon Hill and Ralf Schumacher first and second, with Sauber's Jean Alesi elevated to third when Eddie Irvine fell foul of the wet conditions. The safety car was called out for a second time after Giancarlo Fisichella slammed into the back of Shinji Nakano and just missed hitting the end of the pit wall. But when the safety car pulled off, Hill held on to resist his team-mate and send team boss Eddie Jordan skipping with delight down the pit lane. At the 127th time of asking, Jordan had won a Grand Prix.

HILL ESCAPES: As Hakkinen and Schumacher clash at the second start, Damon Hill makes a break on what proved to be a great day for Jordan

ITALIAN GP

FERRARI'S DREAM DAY

RACE RESULTS
ROUND 14 AT MONZA, SEPTEMBER 14, 1998
(AFTER 53 LAPS)

Pos	Driver	Team
1	MICHAEL SCHUMACHER	Ferrari
2	EDDIE IRVINE	Ferrari
3	RALF SCHUMACHER	Jordan
4	MIKA HAKKINEN	McLaren
5	JEAN ALESI	Sauber
6	DAMON HILL	Jordan

FASTEST LAP: Hakkinen, 1m 25.139s (151.61mph/243.98km/h)
WEATHER CONDITIONS: Warm, dry and sunny

McLaren was expected to dominate at Monza but it all went wrong, and Ferrari delighted the *tifosi* with a one-two, victory putting Michael Schumacher equal on points with Mika Hakkinen with just two races to run.

Monza, the experts said, would be a McLaren benefit. The track was tailor-made to get the best out of designer Adrian Newey's fabulously aerodynamic chassis and Mercedes's lusty engine. Pre-event testing backed this up, with the *tifosi*'s new number-one enemy David Coulthard lapping easily fastest at Monza in the week before the race. Michael Schumacher was seventh fastest, over a second behind the Scot.

Tension from the aftermath of their collision at Spa-Francorchamps threatened to overshadow the Italian Grand Prix, but Formula One ringmaster Bernie Ecclestone encouraged them to talk it out and shake hands before going out on to the track. Then, as if someone were controlling the weather in the interests of keeping the title-race going, it rained. With the track still damp at the start of the qualifying hour, everyone sat it out until there were just 25 minutes left before going out on their precious rubber. And, lo and behold, Michael Schumacher snatched pole position as the McLaren men hit traffic on the final fliers. Jacques Villeneuve started second, Hakkinen third and Coulthard fourth. Belgian GP-winner Damon Hill languished in 14th.

Dreams of holding off the superior McLarens for as long as possible came to nought when Schumacher made a dreadful start, and immediately found himself down in fifth behind Hakkinen, Coulthard, Irvine and Villeneuve. Before the lap was out he was up to fourth, and soon afterward Irvine let him through to third. But the McLarens were clear. Then Coulthard took the lead and pulled clear as Schumacher edged up to Hakkinen's tail. The

German then won a double jackpot as the two of them hit a wall of smoke from Nakano's blown engine. Hakkinen lifted off and Schumacher dived by. But this wasn't for second place, but for the lead, as Coulthard had also pulled over with a dead engine.

Once he had taken the lead, Michael Schumacher controlled the race. However, Hakkinen closed in after their pit stops until a braking problem pitched him into a gravel trap.

He rejoined, but further damage meant he was powerless to stop Irvine and Ralf Schumacher going by. And fourth place meant that he and Michael Schumacher were equal on points with just two races to go.

The most unusual reason for retirement came from Johnny Herbert, who spun off when an errant pair of pliers jammed his pedals... Team-mate Jean Alesi was more fortunate and finished fifth, just ahead of Damon Hill.

DREAM RESULT: Michael Schumacher and Eddie Irvine answered Italy's prayers with a famous one-two for Ferrari after both McLarens failed

LUXEMBOURG GP

HAKKINEN PROVES A POINT

RACE RESULTS

ROUND 15 AT NURBURGRING,
SEPTEMBER 27, 1998

(AFTER 67 LAPS) 1ST ROUND

Pos	Driver	Team
1	MIKA HAKKINEN	McLaren
2	MICHAEL SCHUMACHER	Ferrari
3	DAVID COULTHARD	McLaren
4	EDDIE IRVINE	Ferrari
5	HEINZ-HARALD FRENTZEN	Williams
6	GIANCARLO FISICHELLA	Benetton

FASTEST LAP Mika Hakkinen 1m 20.450s
(126.682mph/203.866km/h)
WEATHER CONDITIONS Cool, overcast
and dry

Michael Schumacher thought he had the beating of Mika Hakkinen after his surprise win at Monza, but the Finn fought back off the ropes to score a famous win.

The Ferraris hadn't been expected to race well at Monza, but Schumacher surprised the McLaren men by qualifying on pole and racing to victory. So, when he qualified on pole at the Nurburgring, with team-mate Eddie Irvine alongside, McLaren's worst fears must have been realized.

These fears grew by the second when Hakkinen failed to get past them on the run down to the first corner. Indeed, he ran through the first twister behind Schumacher but was still in third, as Irvine had made another good start and Schumacher another weak one. Before the lap was out, though, Irvine had made a mistake and was down to second. Over the next few laps, it looked like the French GP all over again as the Ulsterman delayed Hakkinen and

David Coulthard while his lord and master escaped into the distance.

However, after 13 laps of trying, he found a way past Irvine at the chicane and set off after Schumacher, who was 8.5 seconds up the road. But Hakkinen was on a mission and brought this deficit down bit by bit. When Schumacher pitted for his first stop on lap 24, the gap was down to 5.8 seconds, but still Hakkinen stayed out and put in some unbelievably fast laps. It only became clear how fast they had been when he pitted on lap 28 and emerged just ahead of a shocked Schumacher.

They ran almost nose-to-tail until half-a-dozen laps before their second pit stops, when Schumacher's car started to corner in ever more lurid fashion and Hakkinen eased clear.

The gap stretched further when the McLaren crew turned Hakkinen around faster than Ferrari serviced Schumacher. And that was that, with Hakkinen controlling the race to the finish. Certainly it returned him to the championship lead – by four points, going into the final race – but it was worth more than that, as it was Hakkinen's first win since the German GP at the start of August, and gave him the confidence that he could win a straight fight with his rival.

Of the supporting act, Coulthard was a distant third, with Irvine a further half a minute behind in fourth, just ahead of the battling trio of Heinz-Harald Frentzen, Giancarlo Fisichella and Alexander Wurz. Ralf Schumacher was unfortunate not to have scored after climbing to fifth before brake failure pitched him off.

THE TITLE RACE: Just when Michael Schumacher thought he had the measure of Hakkinen, the Finn fought back

JAPANESE GP

MIKA RACES TO GLORY

Mika Hakkinen thought that he'd become World Champion when Michael Schumacher stalled on the grid, then was absolutely sure of it when Schumacher had a blow-out later in the race.

RACE RESULTS

ROUND 16 AT SUZUKA
NOVEMBER 1, 1998

(AFTER 51 LAPS)

Pos	Driver	Team
1	MIKA HAKKINEN	McLaren
2	EDDIE IRVINE	Ferrari
3	DAVID COULTHARD	McLaren
4	DAMON HILL	Jordan
5	HEINZ-HARALD FRENTZEN	Williams
6	JACQUES VILLENEUVE	Williams

FASTEST LAP Michael Schumacher 1m 40.190s (125.338mph/210.703km/h)
WEATHER CONDITIONS Warm, dry and sunny

Michael Schumacher travelled to Suzuka knowing that he had to win the Japanese GP to stand a chance of winning the title. Even then, he would probably need Ferrari team-mate Eddie Irvine to come home second to be sure of outstripping Mika Hakkinen. Luckily for Ferrari, Irvine always goes well at what was once his home circuit.

However, when qualifying was over, Irvine was only fourth on the grid and would have to make a cracking start to overhaul the McLarens that lay between him and pole-sitting Schumacher. But then his role changed totally when Schumacher stalled at the second start – the first having been aborted when Jarno Trulli stalled – and so the German driver had to take the third start from the rear of the grid.

Irvine made a great getaway at the start, outstripping David Coulthard who also fell behind Heinz-Harald Frentzen's Williams on the run to the first corner. But Irvine failed to prevent Hakkinen from taking the lead, and could offer little resistance as the Finn edged away.

Schumacher was down, but not out, and climbed from twenty-first to twelfth on the first lap. He kept up his optimistic charge until being caught behind Damon Hill's Jordan on lap 5. But Hill was fighting for fifth with Jacques Villeneuve and was not keen to cede position, staying ahead of Schumacher for the next eight laps before making his first pit stop.

Driving a blinder, though, he made it up to third place by lap 32 and was due to pit again when he hit debris from an accident at the chicane between Toranosuke Takagi and Esteban Tuero, and suffered a blow-out at the end of the main straight. There was no chance

TITLE SETTLER: Schumacher stalls and the title is heading Hakkinen's way

of returning to the pits, and Schumacher could only pull on to the grass verge and retire. This meant that the title was Hakkinen's, whether he finished or not. But, whistling as he went, he did win the race, from Irvine and Coulthard, with Hill taking fourth place from Frentzen at the chicane on the final lap – much to the fury of Williams boss Patrick Head.

It seemed to take a while to sink in, even though he ran the last 20 laps sure that he was champion. But then, after being congratulated by a sporting Schumacher, Hakkinen went loopy, running around parc fermé like a madman before being guided away to meet the press. Gulping in front of the cameras, he struggled to take in the reality of it all.

NOTE
Drivers are listed according to their finishing position in each race.

SCORING SYSTEM
First, 10 points; second, 6 points; third, 4 points; fourth, 3 points; fifth, 2 points; sixth, 1 point.

	DRIVER	(Nat)	CAR-ENGINE	March 8, Melbourne	March 29, Interlagos	April 12, Buenos Aires	April 26, Imola	May 10, Barcelona
1	Mika Hakkinen	(FIN)	McLaren-Mercedes MP4/13	1PF	1PF	2	R	1PF
2	Michael Schumacher	(GER)	Ferrari F300	R	3	1	2F	3
3	David Coulthard	(GBR)	McLaren-Mercedes MP4/13	2	2	6P	1P	2
4	Eddie Irvine	(GBR)	Ferrari F300	4	8	3	3	R
5	Jacques Villeneuve	(CAN)	Williams-Mecachrome FW20	5	7	R	4	6
6	Damon Hill	(GBR)	Jordan-Mugen Honda 198	8	D	8	10*	R
7	Heinz-Harald Frentzen	(GER)	Williams-Mecachrome FW20	3	5	9	5	8
	Alexander Wurz	(AUT)	Benetton-Mecachrome B198	7	4	4F	R	4
9	Giancarlo Fisichella	(ITA)	Benetton-Mecachrome B198	R	6	7	R	R
10	Ralf Schumacher	(GER)	Jordan-Mugen Honda 198	R	R	R	7	11
11	Jean Alesi	(FRA)	Sauber-Petronas C17	R	9	5	6	10
12	Rubens Barrichello	(BRA)	Stewart-Ford SF-2	R	R	10	R	5
13	Pedro Diniz	(BRA)	Arrows A19	R	R	R	R	R
	Mika Salo	(FIN)	Arrows A19	R	R	R	9	R
15	Johnny Herbert	(GBR)	Sauber-Petronas C17	6	R	R	R	7
	Jan Magnussen	(DEN)	Stewart-Ford SF-2	R	10	R	R	12
	Jarno Trulli	(ITA)	Prost-Peugeot AP01	R	R	11	R	9
-	Olivier Panis	(FRA)	Prost-Peugeot AP01	9	R	R	11*	16*
-	Ricardo Rosset	(BRA)	Tyrrell-Ford 026	R	R	14	R	NQ
-	Toranosuke Takagi	(JAP)	Tyrrell-Ford 026	R	R	12	R	13
-	Shinji Nakano	(JAP)	Minardi-Ford M198	R	R	13	R	14
-	Esteban Tuero	(ARG)	Minardi-Ford M198	R	R	R	8	15
-	Jos Verstappen	(HOL)	Stewart-Ford SF-2	-	-	-	-	-

	CONSTRUCTOR						
1	McLaren-Mercedes	16	16	7	10	16
2	Ferrari	3	4	14	10	4
3	Williams-Mecachrome	6	2		5	1
4	Jordan-Mugen Honda	-	-	-	-	-
5	Benetton-Mecachrome	-	4	3	-	3
6	Sauber-Petronas	1	-	2	1	-
7	Arrows	-	-	-	-	-
8	Stewart-Ford	-	-	-	-	2
9	Prost-Peugeot	-	-	-	-	-
-	Minardi-Ford	-	-	-	-	-
-	Tyrrell-Ford	-	-	-	-	-

May 24, Monaco	June 7, Montreal	June 28, Magny-Cours	July 12, Silverstone	July 26, A1-Ring	August 2, Hockenheim	August 16, Hungaroring	August 30, Spa-Francorchamps	September 13, Monza	September 27, Nurburgring	November 1, Suzuka	Points total
1PF	R	3P	2P	1	1P	6P	RP	4F	1F	1	100
10	1F	1	1F	3	5	1F	RF	1P	2P	RPF	86
R	RP	6F	R	2F	2F	2	7	R	3	3	56
3	3	2	3	4	8	R	R	2	4	2	47
5	10	4	7	6	3	3	R	R	8	6	21
8	R	R	R	7	4	4	1	6	9	4	20
R	R	15*	R	R	9	5	4	7	5	5	17
R	4	5	4	9	11	R	R	R	7	9	17
2	2	9	5	RP	7	8	R	8	6	8	16
R	R	16	6	5	6	9	2	3	R	R	14
12*	R	7	R	R	10	7	3	5	10	7	9
R	5	10	R	R	R	R	NS	10	11	R	4
6	9	14	R	R	R	11	5	R	R	R	3
4	R	13	R	R	14	R	NS	R	14	R	3
7	R	8	R	8	R	10	R	R	R	10	1
R	6	-	-	-	-	-	-	-	-	-	1
R	R	R	R	10	12	R	6	13	R	12	1
R	R	11	R	R	15	12	NS	R	12	11	
NQ	8	R	R	12	NP	NQ	NS	12	R	NQ	
11	R	R	9	R	13	14	R	9	16	R	
9	7	17*	8	11	R	15	8	R	15	R	
R	R	R	R	R	16	R	R	11	R	R	
-	-	12	R	R	R	13	R	R	13	R	

SYMBOLS P denotes pole position; F denotes fastest lap; R denotes retired from race; * Denotes classified but not running at finish; NC denotes not classified (ie. still running at end of race, but having covered insufficient distance); NS denotes did not start; NQ denotes did not qualify; NP denotes did not practice; D denotes disqualified; - denotes did not enter race.

May 24, Monaco	June 7, Montreal	June 28, Magny-Cours	July 12, Silverstone	July 26, A1-Ring	August 2, Hockenheim	August 16, Hungaroring	August 30, Spa-Francorchamps	September 13, Monza	September 27, Nurburgring	November 1, Suzuka	Points total
10	-	5	6	16	16	7	-	3	14	14	156
4	14	16	14	7	2	10	-	16	9	6	133
2	-	3	-	1	4	6	3	-	2	3	38
-	-	-	1	2	4	3	16	5	-	3	34
6	9	2	5	-	-	-	-	-	1	-	33
-	-	-	-	-	-	-	4	2	-	-	10
4	-	-	-	-	-	-	2	-	-	-	6
-	-	3	-	-	-	-	-	-	-	-	5
-	-	-	-	-	-	-	1	-	-	-	1
-	-	-	-	-	-	-	-	-	-	-	0
-	-	-	-	-	-	-	-	-	-	-	0

FORMULA ONE RECORDS

Most Grand Prix starts

DRIVERS

256	Riccardo Patrese (ITA)	144	Emerson Fittipaldi (BRA)
210	Gerhard Berger (AUT)	135	Jean-Pierre Jarier (FRA)
208	Andrea de Cesaris (ITA)	132	Eddie Cheever (USA)
204	Nelson Piquet (BRA)		Clay Regazzoni (SUI)
199	Alain Prost (FRA)	129	Johnny Herbert (GBR)
194	Michele Alboreto (ITA)	128	Mario Andretti (USA)
187	Nigel Mansell (GBR)	126	Jack Brabham (AUS)
176	Graham Hill (GBR)	123	Ronnie Peterson (SWE)
175	Jacques Laffite (FRA)	119	Pierluigi Martini (ITA)
171	Niki Lauda (AUT)	118	Michael Schumacher
163	Thierry Boutsen (BEL)		(GER)
161	Ayrton Senna (BRA)	116	Jacky Ickx (BEL)
158	Martin Brundle (GBR)		Alan Jones (AUS)
152	John Watson (GBR)	114	Keke Rosberg (FIN)
151	Jean Alesi (FRA)		Patrick Tambay (FRA)
149	Rene Arnoux (FRA)	112	Mika Hakkinen (FIN)
147	Derek Warwick (GBR)		Denny Hulme (NZL)
146	Carlos Reutemann (ARG)		Jody Scheckter (RSA)

CONSTRUCTORS

603	Ferrari	394	Brabham	221	Minardi
490	Lotus	359	Prost	197	BRM
476	McLaren	321	Arrows	132	Osella
418	Tyrrell	267	Benetton	130	Jordan
395	Williams	230	March	129	Cooper

> **FOUR-TIME CHAMPION: Alain Prost scored 51 wins and four titles before he quit to run a team.**

Most wins

DRIVERS

51	Alain Prost (FRA)		Carlos Reutemann (ARG)
41	Ayrton Senna (BRA)	11	Jacques Villeneuve (CDN)
33	Michael Schumacher (GER)	10	Gerhard Berger (AUT)
31	Nigel Mansell (GBR)		James Hunt (GBR)
27	Jackie Stewart (GBR)		Ronnie Peterson (SWE)
25	Jim Clark (GBR)		Jody Scheckter (RSA)
	Niki Lauda (AUT)	9	Mika Hakkinen (FIN)
24	Juan Manuel Fangio (ARG)	8	Denny Hulme (NZL)
23	Nelson Piquet (BRA)		Jacky Ickx (BEL)
22	Damon Hill (GBR)	7	Rene Arnoux (FRA)
16	Stirling Moss (GBR)	6	Tony Brooks (GBR)
14	Jack Brabham (AUS)		Jacques Laffite (FRA)
	Emerson Fittipaldi (BRA)		Riccardo Patrese (FRA)
	Graham Hill (GBR)		Jochen Rindt (AUT)
13	Alberto Ascari (ITA)		John Surtees (GBR)
12	Mario Andretti (USA)		Gilles Villeneuve (CDN)
	Alan Jones (AUS)		

CONSTRUCTORS

119	Ferrari	15	Renault	2	Honda
116	McLaren	10	Alfa Romeo	1	Eagle
102	Williams	9	Ligier		Hesketh
79	Lotus		Maserati		Jordan
35	Brabham		Matra		Penske
27	Benetton		Mercedes		Porsche
23	Tyrrell		Vanwall		Shadow
17	BRM	3	March		
16	Cooper		Wolf		

Most wins in one season

DRIVERS

9	Nigel Mansell (GBR) 1992
	Michael Schumacher (GER) 1995
8	Mika Hakkinen (FIN) 1998
	Damon Hill (GBR) 1996
	Ayrton Senna (BRA) 1988
	Michael Schumacher (GER) 1994
7	Jim Clark (GBR) 1963
	Alain Prost (FRA) 1984
	Alain Prost (FRA) 1988
	Alain Prost (FRA) 1993
	Ayrton Senna (BRA) 1991

	Jacques Villeneuve (CDN) 1997
6	Mario Andretti (USA) 1978
	Alberto Ascari (ITA) 1952
	Jim Clark (GBR) 1965
	Juan Manuel Fangio (ARG) 1954
	Damon Hill (GBR) 1994
	James Hunt (GBR) 1976
	Nigel Mansell (GBR) 1987
	Michael Schumacher (GER) 1998
	Ayrton Senna (BRA) 1989
	Ayrton Senna (BRA) 1990

CONSTRUCTORS

15	McLaren 1988		Williams 1997	Ferrari 1979
12	McLaren 1984	7	Ferrari 1952	Ferrari 1990
	Williams 1996		Ferrari 1953	Ferrari 1998
11	Benetton 1995		Lotus 1963	Lotus 1965
10	McLaren 1989		Lotus 1973	Lotus 1970
	Williams 1992		Tyrrell 1971	Matra 1969
	Williams 1993		Williams 1991	McLaren 1976
9	McLaren 1998		Williams 1994	McLaren 1985
	Williams 1986	6	Alfa Romeo 1950	McLaren 1990
	Williams 1987		Alfa Romeo 1951	Vanwall 1958
8	Benetton 1994		Cooper 1960	Williams 1980
	Lotus 1978		Ferrari 1975	Vanwall 1958
	McLaren 1991		Ferrari 1976	Williams 1980

Most consecutive wins

9	Alberto Ascari (ITA) 1952/53		Damon Hill (GBR) 1995/96
5	Jack Brabham (AUS) 1960		Alain Prost (FRA) 1993
	Jim Clark (GBR) 1965		Jochen Rindt (AUT) 1970
	Nigel Mansell (GBR) 1992		Michael Schumacher (GER) 1994
4	Jack Brabham (AUS) 1966		
	Jim Clark (GBR) 1963		Ayrton Senna (BRA) 1988
	Juan Manuel Fangio (ARG) 1953/54		Ayrton Senna (BRA) 1991

PODIUM PARTY TIME: Ayrton Senna lets the
Champagne fly after one of his 41 Grand Prix wins

Grand Prix starts without a win

208	Andrea de Cesaris (ITA)	97	Chris Amon (NZL)
158	Martin Bundle (GBR)		Rubens Barrichello (BRA)
147	Derek Warwick (GBR)	95	Ukyo Katayama (JAP)
135	Jean-Pierre Jarier (FRA)	93	Ivan Capelli (ITA)
132	Eddie Cheever (USA)	84	Jonathan Palmer (GBR)
119	Pierluigi Martini (ITA)	82	Marc Surer (SUI)
109	Philippe Alliot (FRA)	81	Eddie Irvine (GBR)

F1

FORMULA ONE
RECORDS
124

Greatest number of fastest laps

DRIVERS

41	Alain Prost (FRA)	19	Damon Hill (GBR)
33	Michael Schumacher (GER)		Ayrton Senna (BRA)
30	Nigel Mansell (GBR)	15	Clay Regazzoni (SUI)
28	Jim Clark (GBR)		Jackie Stewart (GBR)
25	Niki Lauda (AUT)	14	Jacky Ickx (BEL)
23	Juan Manuel Fangio (ARG)	13	Alan Jones (AUS)
	Nelson Piquet (BRA)		Riccardo Patrese (ITA)
21	Gerhard Berger (AUT)	12	Rene Arnoux (FRA)
20	Stirling Moss (GBR)	11	Alberto Ascari (ITA)
			John Surtees (GBR)

CONSTRUCTORS

132	Ferrari	20	Tyrrell	12	Matra
110	Williams	18	Renault	11	Ligier
80	McLaren	15	BRM	9	Mercedes
71	Lotus		Maserati	7	March
40	Brabham	14	Alfa Romeo	6	Vanwall
35	Benetton	13	Cooper		

Most pole positions

DRIVERS

65	Ayrton Senna (BRA)	14	Alberto Ascari (ITA)
33	Jim Clark (GBR)		James Hunt (GBR)
	Alain Prost (FRA)		Ronnie Peterson (SWE)
32	Nigel Mansell (GBR)	13	Jack Brabham (AUS)
28	Juan Manuel Fangio (ARG)		Graham Hill (GBR)
24	Niki Lauda (AUT)		Jacky Ickx (BEL)
	Nelson Piquet (BRA)		Jacques Villeneuve (CDN)
20	Damon Hill (GBR)	12	Gerhard Berger (AUT)
	Michael Schumacher (GER)	10	Mika Hakkinen (FIN)
18	Mario Andretti (USA)		Jochen Rindt (AUT)
	Rene Arnoux (FRA)	8	David Coulthard (GBR)
17	Jackie Stewart (GBR)		Riccardo Patrese (ITA)
16	Stirling Moss (GBR)		John Surtees (GBR)

CONSTRUCTORS

124	Ferrari	14	Tyrrell	7	Vanwall
108	Williams	12	Alfa Romeo	5	March
107	Lotus	11	BRM	4	Matra
92	McLaren		Cooper	3	Shadow
39	Brabham	10	Maserati	2	Lancia
31	Renault	9	Ligier	1	Jordan
16	Benetton	8	Mercedes		

IN ONE SEASON, DRIVERS

14	Nigel Mansell (GBR) 1992		Ronnie Peterson (SWE) 1973
13	Alain Prost (FRA) 1993		
	Ayrton Senna (BRA) 1988		Nelson Piquet (BRA) 1984
	Ayrton Senna (BRA)1989	8	Mario Andretti (USA) 1978
10	Ayrton Senna (BRA) 1990		James Hunt (GBR) 1976
	Jacques Villeneuve (CDN) 1997		Nigel Mansell (GBR) 1987
			Ayrton Senna (BRA) 1986
9	Mika Hakkinen (FIN) 1998		Ayrton Senna (BRA) 1991
	Damon Hill (GBR) 1996	7	Mario Andretti (USA) 1977
	Niki Lauda (AUT) 1974		Jim Clark (GBR) 1963
	Niki Lauda (AUT) 1975		Ayrton Senna (BRA) 1985

IN ONE SEASON, CONSTRUCTORS

15	McLaren 1988		Williams 1996
	McLaren 1989	11	Williams 1997
	Williams 1992	10	Ferrari 1974
	Williams 1993		Lotus 1973
12	Lotus 1978		McLaren 1991
	McLaren 1990		Renault 1982
	McLaren 1998	9	Brabham 1984
	Williams 1987		Ferrari 1975
	Williams 1995		

GOING FOR GOLD: Niki Lauda powers his Ferrari towards his first world championship in 1975

Most points

(this figure is gross tally, ie. including scores that were later dropped)

DRIVERS

798.5	Alain Prost (FRA)	289	Graham Hill (GBR)
614	Ayrton Senna (BRA)	281	Emerson Fittipaldi (BRA)
526	Michael Schumacher (GER)		Riccardo Patrese (ITA)
485.5	Nelson Piquet (BRA)	277.5	Juan Manuel Fangio (ARG)
482	Nigel Mansell (GBR)	274	Jim Clark (GBR)
420.5	Niki Lauda (AUT)	261	Jack Brabham (AUS)
385	Gerhard Berger (AUT)	255	Jody Scheckter (ZA)
360	Jackie Stewart (GBR)	248	Denny Hulme (NZL)
353	Damon Hill (GBR)	235	Jean Alesi (FRA)
310	Carlos Reutemann (ARG)	228	Jacques Laffite (FRA)

CONSTRUCTORS

2226.5	Ferrari	439	BRM			Matra
2204.5	McLaren	411	Prost	79		Sauber
1960.5	Williams	333	Cooper			Wolf
1352	Lotus	312	Renault	67.5		Shadow
854	Brabham	171.5	March	57		Vanwall
831.5	Benetton	156	Arrows			
617	Tyrrell	155	Jordan			

ONE OF THE GREATS: Jim Clark raced to a pair of world drivers' titles for Lotus in 1963 and 1965

Most drivers' titles

5	Juan Manuel Fangio (ARG)	Mika Hakkinen (FIN)
4	Alain Prost (FRA)	Mike Hawthorn (GBR)
3	Jack Brabham (AUS)	Damon Hill (GBR)
	Niki Lauda (AUT)	Phil Hill (USA)
	Nelson Piquet (BRA)	Denis Hulme (NZL)
	Ayrton Senna (BRA)	James Hunt (GBR)
	Jackie Stewart (GBR)	Alan Jones (AUS)
2	Alberto Ascari (ITA)	Nigel Mansell (GBR)
	Jim Clark (GBR)	Jochen Rindt (AUT)
	Emerson Fittipaldi (BRA)	Keke Rosberg (FIN)
	Graham Hill (GBR)	Jody Scheckter (RSA)
	Michael Schumacher (GER)	John Surtees (GBR)
1	Mario Andretti (USA)	Jacques Villeneuve (CDN)
	Giuseppe Farina (ITA)	

Most constructors' titles

9	Williams	2	Brabham		Matra
8	Ferrari		Cooper		Tyrrell
	McLaren	1	Benetton		Vanwall
7	Lotus		BRM		

1999 FIA FORMULA ONE

F1

			March 7, Australian GP	March 28, Argentina GP	April 11, Brazilian GP	May 2, San Marino GP	May 16, Monaco GP	May 30, Spanish GP	June 13, Canadian GP
1 McLaren	Mika Hakkinen	(FIN)							
2 McLaren	David Coulthard	(GBR)							
3 Ferrari	Michael Schumacher	(GER)							
4 Ferrari	Eddie Irvine	(GBR)							
5 Jordan	Heinz-Harald Frentzen	(GER)							
6 Jordan	Damon Hill	(GBR)							
7 Benetton	Giancarlo Fisichella	(ITA)							
8 Benetton	Alexander Wurz	(AUT)							
9 Williams	Ralf Schumacher	(GER)							
10 Williams	Alessandro Zanardi	(ITA)							
11 Sauber	Jean Alesi	(FRA)							
12 Sauber	Pedro Diniz	(BRA)							
14 Stewart	Rubens Barrcihello	(BRA)							
15 Stewart	Johnny Herbert	(GBR)							
16 Arrows	Mika Salo	(FIN)							
17 Arrows	Toranosuke Takagi	(JAP)							
18 Prost	Olivier Panis	(FRA)							
19 Prost	Jarno Trulli	(ITA)							
20 Minardi	Shinji Nakano	(JAP)							
21 Minardi	Esteban Tuero	(ARG)							
22 BAR	Jacques Villeneuve	(CAN)							
23 BAR	Ricardo Zonta	(BRA)							

WORLD CHAMPIONSHIP

June 27, French GP	July 11, British GP	July 25, Austrian GP	August 1, German GP	August 15, Hungarian GP	August 29, Belgian GP	September 12, Italian GP	September 26, European GP	October 17, Malaysian GP	October 31, Japanese GP

WILL SCHUEY BE CRYING IN 1999?: Michael Schumacher will be gunning for his third world title with Ferrari

The publishers would like to thank the following sources for their kind permission to reproduce the pictures in this book:

Allsport UK Ltd/124, 125; Michael Cooper 5, 6/7, 10/11, 13, 14, 16, 17, 19, 24, 27, 33, 36, 39, 40, 41, 47, 54, 64/65, 66, 67, 68, 70, 77, 79, 81, 84, 88, 95, 103, 108, 115, 116, 117, 128; John Gigichi 8; Mike Hewitt 72; Jamie Squire 22; Tom Shaw 92, 93, 102, 103br; Michael King 122; Clive Mason 98, 99; Pascal Rondeau 31, 69, 71, 90, 94, 106, 123; Jamie Squire 57; David Taylor 110; Mark Thompson 2/3, 4tl, 5, 15, 20, 26, 30, 32, 43, 58, 73, 75, 76, 85, 100/101, 102, 107, 113, 119; Vandystadt 74, 86, 87; Empics/John Marsh 21, 38, 112; Steve Mitchell 18, 56; LAT/9, 12, 29, 34, 35, 37, 42, 78, 91, 109; Charles Coates 51; Martin Elford 104; Sporting Pictures (UK) Ltd/1, 4bl, 23, 25, 28, 44, 45, 46, 48, 49, 50, 52, 53, 55, 59, 80, 82, 83, 89, 111, 118, 120; Sutton Motorsports 96, 97.

Every effort has been made to acknowledge correctly and contact the source and/or copyright holder of each picture, and Carlton Books Limited apologises for any unintentional errors or omissions which will be corrected in future editions of this book.